PROSE & LORE

PROSE & LORE

Issue 2

Spring/Summer 2013

RED UMBRELLA PROJECT

EDITOR & PUBLISHER   Audacia Ray
ASSOCIATE PUBLISHER   Danielle Sipple
COVER & LOGO DESIGN   Shawn Tamaribuchi

CONTENTS

ACKNOWLEDGMENTS

We are grateful for the support that was generously provided by New York Women's Foundation, New York Foundation, and Association for Women's Rights in Development, which has made the Red Umbrella Project memoir workshop, the Red Umbrella Diaries, and *Prose & Lore*, as well as other RedUP programs, possible. Thanks also to the New School for providing space for us to hold our memoir workshops and to Jessica Mannion for her copy edits.

INTRODUCTION
Audacia Ray

Writers are often portrayed as solitary creatures, typing or scrawling away in tiny, dark rooms. For writers, this solo suffering to bring art into the world is often cast as a heroic process. People who trade or sell sex are also often portrayed as solitary creatures. I can't count how many times I've seen an image in a newspaper or on a news show of a person in a short skirt leaning into a rolled-down car window, backlit by headlights, maybe some red-tinted light. But this solo act is never regarded as anything near heroic.

I'd like to propose that neither writing nor trading sex are heroic acts. But when people who trade sex get together in a room and share our stories and share our writing with each other—it might be too much to say that's heroic, but it certainly is ground shaking.

I was involved for four years with *Spread*, a magazine by and for sex workers that was independently published starting in March 2005 and released its final issue in January 2011. We got submissions from all over the world from sex workers who wanted to be a part of something created by our community. I have had the great privilege to meet some of the folks who contributed to *Spread* over the years, but the vast majority of the contributors remained physically isolated from the editors and from each other.

Since starting to produce monthly sex worker storytelling events in New York City in 2009, I have had the pleasure of being witness to the stories of dozens of sex workers as they have told them, in their own words, before audiences that were sometimes amused and sometimes horrified by—but always supportive and receptive of—the stories and their tellers.

Telling stories in community—out loud in a room—is a powerful thing. But being a witness is not just about being in the room with someone and hearing their voice shake as they speak their truth. Having stories take up space in the world—in, say, a literary journal—is important too. Within the Red Umbrella Project (RedUP) community in New York, we are trying to create spaces—physical, creative, and emotional—where people who have sold or traded sex can be honest with each other and can develop the skills of writing and telling their stories. In this practice of honesty, we encourage people to own their truths and speak out in ways that feel useful to them. For some people this means performing in our improv storytelling classes before an audience of their peers, for others it means publishing work in this journal, and for still others it manifests as becoming a media spokesperson, telling a story in public, or doing legislative advocacy.

I've been standing among people who sell or trade sex for the better part of ten years now, and this spring, during the eight weeks of RedUP's memoir writing workshop, I felt awed and humbled by the writing everyone produced. I was especially in awe of the kindness and support everyone showed each other in the class, and everyone's willingness to hold the space for each other, when hard but true words were said.

But I also had the same one-on-one conversation with many members of the class. Class members often privately confessed to me that they felt like everyone else in the class was such an amazing writer, so much better than they themselves could be. It both broke and healed my heart to hear this, because it is so hard for us to see value in our own words and experiences, and so easy to see it in those of others.

I've never been more sure that there is inherent value in the life stories of people in the sex trades and that it is important to put these stories out into the world. There is no way to summarize or generalize about the experiences of people in the sex trades. The only way to know anything about the sex trades is to hear and trust the many stories of the people involved in it, and to keep listening, even when the stories offer conflicting viewpoints. We invite you to join us in being a witness to these stories.

Audacia Ray
Editor & Publisher
June 2013

RITA AND TIARA AND THE WEST VILLAGE STROLL
Rita Rachaels

For Tiara and I, working as female transsexual prostitutes was very special. We were challenging and breaking layer after layer of societal rules, governing who you can be and what you can do. At 3 am I am exactly what they want. They come to me; they can't go to their wives. The feeling can only be described as electric.

With high-octane dance music blaring from the radio, we awoke at 10 pm to get ready for the stroll. Tiara began her ritual by selecting a wig. Mine began by shaving all the hair off my body. We were transsexual whores and every single feminine attribute we had we accentuated to the hilt. For Tiara it was her ass and for me it was my legs. We played music so loudly that we had to shout to each other to be heard. Here we were, two magnificent transsexual women, holding our guts and bravery high for the world to see.

When we got to the West Village stroll at 1 am, Tiara took Greenwich Street and I took Washington. Our goodbyes were short. We knew all too well that what we were doing was a far cry from Friday night bowling. And we were thinking only that we did not want to end up in the trunk of a car or Central Booking by night's end.

The air on the stroll is like an unbelievably fine mist, no matter the weather, and it made me feel assured that the NYPD would not set fire to the blanket of surveillance they covered me with. Nonetheless, I was also acutely aware that the police could arrest me at any time. I reached my destination each time my heels hit the pavement and all of my plans could be found on the balls of my feet.

Every few hours, Tiara would walk over to say "Hi." I can't tell you how beautiful she was—and tall—six three. Her skin was a gorgeous deep bronze and her eyes were as huge and as brilliant as search lights. Tiara was young and she had come from a hellish world of savage beatings and zero love. I emptied all my heart to her. She made me feel so wonderfully alive. We were the world's proudest misfits. When our nighttime sky began to lighten with the dawn, we both knew that we were being forced into a world that never wanted us. We knew that we had stolen a part of our lives and a piece of ourselves. When we walked off the stroll, the gentleness and simplicity of our holding hands was the refuge we made for each other. It was the greatest feeling and privilege I have ever had. Riding the subway home, people stared at us as if we were vermin, dirty and mean. We lived so much in our vulnerability; how could we be anything but clean?

One night, when Tiara was walking toward me for our customary check-in hello, when she was just across the corner from me, two detectives—a man and a woman—seemed to pop out of nowhere. One put Tiara in handcuffs. Tiara began to cry out, "Why are you arresting me—I didn't do anything!"

The female detective said, "We've been watching you for two hours--we know exactly what you've been doing."

I stood, absolutely frozen, down the block. I was wearing black lingerie and watching Tiara get arrested. I was as still as a drop of honey on the face of a grizzly bear. Then Tiara called out my name, "Rita!" Then again, "Rita, come here!"

I couldn't believe it. I thought, if I go over to her I'll be arrested. Then I thought, if Tiara is getting busted, then so will I. I crossed the street and the male detective said, casually, "How are you, Rita?"

I said, "Very well, thank you, Officer."

Now he was searching Tiara's bag, peering into it with a pen light. Tiara had a knife in her bag but he didn't see it. When he was done with the search, he placed Tiara's bag on the pavement. Tiara said to me, "Take my bag—I won't need it in jail." I looked at the detective and he motioned for me to go. I picked up Tiara's bag, and off I went.

As I started to cross the street, Tiara called out again, "Wait, Rita, come here." So I went back to her again. She said, "Give me twenty bucks from my purse. I need it for commissary." I dug through her bag for it, and handed her the twenty dollars. The officers motioned for me to leave, and I took off down the block. I got rid of the knife as soon as I could without them seeing me.

As I was walking home with Tiara's bag, I realized that I loved her. When I got home I called the Sixth Precinct, which is where we had been working. A lady officer answered the phone. I asked her to pass a message along to Tiara that I loved her and would wait for her. The officer said she would, and I thanked her. Tiara and I had just met a week and a half earlier and I wanted her to know what I had just realized. The officer passed my message along. This is how the most powerful love relationship I ever had founds its beginning.

LOOSE LIPS SINK
Danielle

It's someone's job just to name them all. There were specific categories.

The innocent ones: Daylight Goddess, Playful Rose, Juniper Berry.

The cool ones: Coffee Bean, Tart Cherry, Red Velvet.

The devilish ones: Cruella Deville, Blood Vampire, Broken Heart.

Each one of them, very specific to their purpose. Some stayed on longer than others for the fear of a memory slip, a trail of where they had been would have been devastating to them, not really me so much.

All I would have to do is re-apply.

Some were meant to be rubbed off, a smearing of passion, a moment of energy that was shared between two people. An impermanent grin that only two people could share.

I had so many I couldn't keep track of them, really. I would put one in my pocket and halfway through the night, I would shout, "Damn it!" as I searched in my empty pocket or purse or anything for the container that wasn't there. The color on my lips stated who I was, so when I was without the cool liveliness of Red Velvet, who was I, really?

Unconsciously, I compartmentalized my makeup in the same manner that I sorted my life. In order to process my work identity in a solid way, and maintain a sense of who I really was when I had my street clothes on, well, I just wore different lipstick.

I don't know when I discovered Juniper Berry, but it fit when I worked. It was pale enough that when I accidentally grazed my lips against a piece of skin that was blank as an empty canvas begging to be marked by the heart shaped curvatures of my cooing, the memory of the color shade would fade quickly. It matched the natural hue of my lips so it brightened them a bit, brought out the happiness, even if it was hidden deep that day. Even if the smiles never came as quickly as I tried to recall them, Juniper Berry would help with that.

Thank god those rooms were dark.

I would never be caught in the outside world wearing Juniper Berry. It screamed innocence in a way that was deafeningly boring when the lights were bright overhead and the sun shone bright. I was not this color outside the dark walls of my working world.

Within in the safety of work, these four walls holding my façade together, I could play up the innocence a bit, in hopes that, for a moment, it was believable, because nothing about the way I looked screamed innocent. I was tattooed and pierced, with shorter hair than most of my fellow workers. When many clients came equipped with the idea of cute innocent girls devoid of anything seemingly alternative about them, I had many strikes against me. The world of bodywork was very specific, and I was displaced.

So I made up for it when I could. My lipstick, for starts.

In the outside world, I had much more fun. I wore my color like a badge of honor, dismantling the eyes around, using a subtle fury that could not be contained.

I wore red, I wore dark purple, I wore colors that stabbed you silently in the heart.

If at work I tried to curb my heartbreaker status for the aid of encouraging repeat appointments, in the world outside I played up the status as a shield. I was proudly a heartbreaker and my lipstick screamed my stance on the whole manner.

An armor from everyone trying to break my heart constantly.

My favorite was Cruella. It was a fat pencil that rolled off matte and flat. I could channel my youthful sensibility and practice on my lips, for I had practiced for years on sheets of paper delightfully glued to the floor. I was born ready to flag my lips red and glaring.

Stay within the lines. Fill in the area with even strokes. Don't break the tip.
I had practiced for this all my life.

Cruella allowed me to tap into my devilish side, to explore my need to command my own world, when my freedom wasn't bound to my need to pay bills and succeed in getting another booking. My freedom in my lipstick dictated who I was in that given moment. I could have been anyone, but I chose who I was by the color I wore.

If I ever forgot for a moment, all I had to do was look in the mirror and by the color of my lips, I could settle into who I was.

Juniper Berry lying down and Cruella walking outside. It was a deadly combination, which I didn't carry lightly.

THE PARK ROYAL
Gerry Visco

"We need more money," Bob told me, standing in the doorway of the living room, spinning vinyl on the turntables and turning the knob on the mixer, blending trippy disco mixes from the imported EPs he'd bought at Downstairs Records and taking an occasional hit from the joint resting in an ashtray next to the stereo. Wearing only BVDs, he was handsome, with intense blue eyes, two days of blond stubble on his cleft chin, and that childish pug nose. Bob hadn't left the house since he'd been out to buy the records three days earlier and the place reeked of reefer. "Turn the beat around, got to hear percussion!" Vicki Sue Robinson sang, the music blaring, heavy on the bass. My apartment was like a disco all day and a lot of the night, too, though we lowered the music after midnight since New York City had noise laws. I'd paid for the stack of records, as usual. And let's not forget about the rent, the groceries, the utility bills, and most of the other expenses.

"OK, but you could put your ad back in?! I'm not the only one who can hustle, my dear!" I told him, collapsing on the black fake fur chaise lounge. "Not only do you not work, you don't clean up, either." I never hesitated to talk tough, but in the long run, it did no good. I let Bob get away with not working, not cleaning up, and having temper tantrums because, unfortunately, I'd become infatuated, even though he was gay. It all started out when we met at Cambridge Community High School, an alternative school in Harvard Square and immediately were drawn to each other.

I was 16 and Bob was 15. Alienated from mainstream culture, we were both experimenting in left-wing politics. It wasn't long before we were out on the streets of Harvard Square at an anti-Viet Nam war protest. We had a lot in common — like being harassed and bullied by the other students from elementary through high school. After a few years of friendship, we moved in together to an apartment in Boston, and inspired by our dreams of becoming famous performers and artists, we moved to New York City, determined to meet Andy Warhol, who we followed closely. Reading *Interview Magazine* in the 1970s provided us with our guidebook to how to be cool and famous. And yes, we did meet Andy and many years later, I wound up writing for *Interview* myself.

That's how we ended up living in The Park Royal, a residential hotel that became a rent-stabilized building on West 73rd Street in October of 1975, after less than a year in Rego Park, Queens. When we'd first moved in together, we'd split everything, but that gradually changed to Bob paying for almost nothing. Then he stopped working altogether—no hustling or any other kind of job. I helped him build up his record collection so he could become a DJ and invested in his photography career by building a dark room and paying for equipment and supplies. Meanwhile, he hadn't applied for any jobs. He always complained about an unfair boss or some impossible situation. For a while, he had a great DJ job at a fancy disco called Cachaça on East 61st Street, but he quit abruptly because of some disagreement about money and the equipment. Bob was always very particular about everything. For example, he would only drink Canada Dry ginger ale and if I dared to bring something else home, he would demand that I go back and get what he wanted right away.

I was used to making the money quick and the customers liked me, but we were always broke. This conversation about our money situation occurred after I'd just returned home myself after a mid-day shopping expedition at Bergdorf Goodman's, one of my favorite department stores. Until arriving home, it had been a relaxing day where I'd dropped a couple of hundred on a new pair of navy and burgundy Charles Jourdain high heels and a Diane Von Furstenberg wrap jersey dress in a snazzy blue print. I stopped at the café for a salade Niçoise. BG's little restaurant was soothing, tranquilly decorated in pristine white. Women who had nothing better to do than shop during the day sat at the counter alone, stuffed shopping bags at their ankles, sipping fresh carrot juice, mulling over whether they'd wisely invested their wads of bills.

Both Bob and I liked to spend my money. It was unfortunate. I'd have to start making more since I hadn't resumed my call girl business since relocating to Manhattan. I don't even remember the details of the move from 63rd Drive in Rego Park to the Upper West Side but Bob and I were relieved to leave the land of bridge and tunnels and excited about finally living in the city after almost a year in New York. An anonymous caller who claimed to be a cop made us very wary, so we left Queens.

When we first moved to the Park Royal, we decided not to turn tricks in the apartment since we were afraid to get into trouble with the management but would instead do "outcalls" where we visited the client. I looked into finding an upscale brothel, though I dreaded working for someone else. We wanted to feel the vibes, get the lay of the land in our new place before we let a stream of men visit. The pre-war building itself was very deluxe, even though the West 70s was sketchy as hell then. Friends would ask us, "Is it safe to come visit you?" Of course it was, but most neighborhoods could be dangerous.

Ever since moving to Manhattan, I've always lived in a doorman building. You never have to worry about losing the key or being raped in the hallway. There was a 24-hour doorman plus a desk clerk, a grouchy old woman with teased white hair called Brenda, who called to announce guests on the house phone. That's where we paid the rent and the staff took messages and gave us mail. The Park Royal had been a residential hotel and continued some of the services—for example, providing linens. The lobby was huge, carpeted, decorated with elaborate chandeliers and marble staircases. There was a men's club at the other end of the lobby and garishly dressed Eastern European Jews went in and out late at night after playing cards, traveling in brightly colored Cadillacs. They were usually rude, never smiling or saying hello, and if they happened to bump into you they never apologized. It was as though they owned the building and who knows, maybe they did. I had heard there was illegal gambling going on in there, but in those days no one cared. On the other side of the building, up the staircase near the elevator, there was a cabaret called The Bushes, referring to the greenery in Central Park. We always snickered at the name because we knew what went on in the bushes—men were getting blown, or at least that's what the name meant to us, especially considering the owner was a good-looking former actor named Richard. He always had a cute young "nephew" or friend staying with him across the hall from us on the eighth floor. They called men like him a "chicken hawk," but nowadays, the boys are called "twinks" not "chickens."

Next to The Bushes, closer to the street, was Anthony's Coiffeurs, a dated salon which catered to old ladies who liked a shampoo, set, dryer, comb out, and hair spray for the helmet hair look. When I was looking for a camp hairdo I went to see Anthony, an Italian-American hairdresser masterful with a teasing comb. He had a mad crush on me, which was not at all reciprocated. Anthony liked to adore a woman wistfully but probably never sealed the deal; at 40-years-old, he still lived with his mother in Brooklyn.

Our new building was located on the landmark block opposite the Dakota, home to John and Yoko, Lauren Bacall, Leonard Bernstein, Roberta Flack, and other big shots. And of course, the legendary location shoot for "Rosemary's Baby" with Mia Farrow had taken place at the Dakota. Actually, Mia lived across the street at the Langley. I sometimes saw her wheeling a baby carriage.

Walking down West 73rd Street, drug dealers were standing on the street corners plying their wares. Muggings were common, and wherever you walked you'd have to look around closely to make sure no one was following. When I took the subway, I often worried someone would stab me from behind. It wasn't so uncommon, after all. And swaggering gay men with sweaters tied over their shoulders were out cruising for sex in the streets. The Nickel Bar, on the corner of 72nd Street and Columbus, always had men congregated out front, crying out "Miss Thing!" and dancing on the sidewalk to the loud beat spilling out whenever the door was opened. The Nickel Bar was nicknamed the "nigger" bar because that's where white guys went to pick up black guys. In those days, gay black men were either very queeny or totally macho Mandingos.

Central Park was always full of gays wearing revealing wife-beater shirts, tightly packed into jeans to show off their "baskets." As they walked toward the Rambles to pick up some trade, if they met a hot number on the way, why wait? The Park was no lush paradise then but rather neglected, littered with trash and raggedy weeds. Jogging wasn't popular until the early 1980s, so usually it was gays, dog owners, and bums wandering around in the meadows. The Upper West Side in those days had few decent stores, just run-down neighborhood places. Forget about yuppie brands in the Pioneer Supermarket, which was mainly patronized and staffed by Latinos.

Big yuppie chain stores were unknown in New York City back then. The population of the neighborhood was pretty diverse, with lower income residents, Latinos, actors, opera singers, musicians, Jewish families, and twenty-somethings. We had almost doubled our rent from Queens, where we paid $250 a month. Now we were paying $450. It was pricey, but the apartment was a huge two-bedroom with two baths. We could afford it as long as I continued to turn tricks.

To avoid getting in trouble with the landlord, I pored through the ads in *Screw* magazine looking for outcall agencies, so I could turn tricks elsewhere. We had friends living downstairs on the sixth floor from Boston who could help. Jimmy was gay, but he lived with his girlfriend Wynn, who'd been a prostitute we knew who lived with our friend Crystal from the Other Side, the notorious gay bar in the Back Bay which photographer Nan Goldin made famous. Both girls had black pimps, which definitely gave them some street cred, though it seemed dangerous to me. Crystal's guy was Calvin, and Wynn was with Rainbow. Wynn was a quiet wan girl who liked to while away the night ironing after the bar. She later moved to New York and moved in with Jimmy and became a couple, even though Jimmy was known to be "gay olé," as we used to say.

Jimmy had begun designing display ads for *Screw* and worked for the Regency outcall agency. They had a thriving business of men and women "escorts" going out to see johns all over the city. The split was fair ——fifty-fifty of $100, which is about what we made when they came to our place, anyway. "You should give them a try. Wynn's been out on a few outcalls and it was easy," Jimmy told me one night when I was visiting them. Of course, it could be dangerous going out to see men in their homes. Hotels were usually safer, but there was always that random dead hooker who'd be found stuffed into a closet at some swanky midtown hotel.

The Regency agency always called the customer back to double-check someone was really at that number and they also checked to see if the guy was listed in the phone book. Unlisted ones could be problematic, but you also had to use your gut sense, and it depended in what neighborhood they lived. We hadn't had the problem of nosy doormen in Queens since our apartment had a buzzer, and our neighbors across the hall were junkies who were always fighting with each other and families who had never spoken to us. Manhattan was totally different but here we were, two 19-year-old and 20-year old kids from the sleepy suburbs of Massachusetts living across the street from John and Yoko.

"Look, I need to buy some new clothes so I can go out and get a job," Bob told me. "I need to look good now that we're in Manhattan. You just went shopping. What about me?" he said, taking a hit of weed as he spoke. I never smoked the stuff but I bought him a nickel bag every day from Chico, the Puerto Rican dealer who worked on the corner of 73rd and Columbus.

"Bob, don't you worry. I'll be making plenty of money when I start acting in motion pictures," I told him, looking in the mirror and modeling my new Charles Jourdan shoes. "I'm going to make it in this world!" I told him, tossing my thick mane of hair like an impatient thoroughbred racehorse. I never realized it was going to be such a long hard road.

SKIN DEEP
Brandon Aguilar

"*This* sticks out more than *that*!" seethed the famed gay porn director as I stood before him, shirtless. He eyed me with a tyrannical scrutiny, a hard hateful gleam pouring from his eyes. Lyle Mucus was a beauty, externally: glowing skin, a muscled statuesque physique, thick expensively-trimmed brown hair. But needlessly cruel to the stable of boys under his wrath, he conducted himself imperiously. A foul-tempered, x-rated empress. It was this behavior that made his ugliness shine forth, his beauty eclipsed by his demeanor. Horrid beestung lips projected outward from his face and made him look gluttonous, a sullen sneer etched on permanently pouting lips. Eyes that radiated contempt for all they saw. It was perhaps this contempt which lent him the balls to come from across the world to launch his gay porn empire. The mask of beauty was a thin facade. The wretched, fetid rot of his soul could not be concealed by all the haute couture and spray-on tan in the world.

He inspected me like a defective slab of meat.

I had come to be looked over so he could cast me in a scene again, so I could continue my lackluster odyssey as a fifth-rate gay porn star. It was only last year I appeared in his raunchy-yet-dull gay porn DVD *Island Slutfest Part 7*. For this performance, one overly generous reviewer online mistakenly praised me as "an anxious bottom who enjoys pleasing his tops." My scene partner for this was the well-known cutiepie stud Herrick Danson (he puts the "hard" into hardcore, they say online).

Herrick was a likable fellow who'd flown all the way from San Francisco to join our ragtag motley family that week. When I complimented him on his tats, he said, "Thanks! They're Bjork's."

The DVD is too boringly traumatic for me watch today, but online the same breathless reviewer noted, "Herrick demands a lot, and Brandon has to get on all fours and exposes his asshole.... Wiggling and writhing from the anal invasion, Brandon has no choice but to take it until Herrick is done!"

Oh, but only if the reality had been as awesome as it all sounds.

Filming *Island Slutfest 7* was no easy task. The scene between myself and Herrick was shot on a warm afternoon in mid-summer, though the scene in the film takes place at night. Rather than simply shooting at a dark hour (because that would be too logical and sane, and I soon found that nothing in porn was ever done with those qualities), the director and crew, impatient for nightfall, decided to "create" night. They did this industriously, boarding up all the windows and doors of the room we were in. The air conditioner hum made too much noise in the background, so they shut it off.

It was me, Herrick, the guy holding the camera, the director egging us on, and another soul or two lurking in the background. They added a burning hot light pointed at us, to film us better. The confined room quickly became an inferno. Herrick and I pummeled, pumped, assaulted, intertwined: the dance of our lusty sweat-drenched sex scene. We tried to maintain the illusion that we were enjoying ourselves. The room filled with an airless, nauseating heat. A queasy look of imminent vomit spread on Herrick's handsome face. "Oh, I think I'm gonna be sick!" Herrick jumped up, broke through the barricaded door, ran out of the room and flung himself into the cool blue waters of the swimming pool out back.

It was all a scorching nightmare. But here I was back at the offices of Mucus Studios, asking for more punishment.

"You must stop drinking Snapple! It's full of sugar," the director bitched, from behind his desk.

"Yea, really," chimed in the bloated so-called porn agent, a useless fat fuck from Florida who procured guys for porn work. Because he worked behind the scenes, he was allowed to be a slovenly pig without enduring body critiques. For in the porn world, with all its hard, beautiful bodies in front of the camera, there is a contingent of hangers-on behind the scenes, who are slovenly, dumpy pigs.

I played along in wide-eyed openness, to assuage the raging ego of our man-diva director, as if he'd shared a helpful insight. "I do a lot of cardio at the gym. I'm addicted to the stairmaster!"

"Cardio is part of it, yes, but also diet," he admonished like the stern schoolmistress he was.

I had been shamed and humiliated in front of a bustling roomful of people. I left with my head hung down. The people in the room watched me go, from a distance of pity and contempt.

The fat porn agent expected me to sleep with him that night, as a freebie, but as I left I said, "Look, after that, I just don't feel too good about myself. I think I'll go home instead."

He understood. I think he pitied me and what I was willing to do for approval.

I went home, fretted and despaired. I emailed Doctor Replica from Chicago.

Dr. Replica: a brilliant photographer/cosmetic doctor that I'd befriended when I lived there. One of his photos graced the cover of one of the books in Oprah's book club selection, a ethereal black and white photograph of baby twins. I thought of him as a great artist, both as a physician and as a photographer.

My general practitioner, Dr. Ken Thomas, who I'd found from his ad in the gay yellow pages, originally referred me to Dr. Replica. Dr. Thomas has an interesting reputation among Chicago gays, if you google him, you may find this: "Ken Thomas, also known as Dr. Feelgood because of his bedside manner and way of pampering customers... has been making the community feel better for decades."

Dr. Thomas used to jack me off with medical-grade lube in the little exam room when I came to see him for a checkup. It was through these jackoff sessions that he noticed my circumcision as a baby had been messed up.

Dr. Replica surgerized it. When I was in my mid-twenties, he performed a genital reconstruction surgery, fixing this botched circumcision. So I called him up and asked about liposuction.

I flew to Chicago for a consultation. Replica's office is on the ground floor of his home, a vast old mansion with dark red wood paneling on the floor and walls. Broken antique dolls line the shelves of his waiting area, an eBay passion of his. "So funny: you have all these maimed dolls everywhere and the patients you see are somewhat the same," I told him.

"Ah, you noticed. Not everybody does," he said. We discussed my options.

Almost prissily, he told me, "I don't like the term 'abs etching.' All surgery leaves scars, but we try to hide the scars." Abs etching is a sort of hip term, which maybe promises a shrink-wrapped six-pack. He wanted me to have realistic expectations, though the scarring would be extremely minimal. He tells me he inserts thin wands under the skin which vacuums out fat. We were planning on transplanting the fat he took from my torso and injecting it to plump up the cheeks on my face and ass. He said he'd do it for $8000, which was a discounted rate since we were quote-unquote friends.

Replica allowed me to pay in installments, like putting cash down on layaway, the retail model of yesteryear. It would've been challenging for me to amass $8000 all at once, though a tremendous amount of money passed through my fingers. And pass it did. Where did it go? I wasn't sure. It costs a lot to survive in New York, surviving and looking good, costs even more. I'd blown my share on facials, pedicures, gym memberships, et cetera.

It's interesting what one can accomplish in a short amount of time when one puts one's mind to it. The summer unfolded like a community service project, everybody pitching in. I viewed it as a fundraiser and watched the sum rise. When I'd get $500 here or there, I'd call Replica's office to tell them to run my card and deduct it. Inch by inch, man by man, the sum rose until the doc had my $8000 and I had my date with destiny.

Replica employed as a front desk girl a ditzy airhead, and he seemed perpetually annoyed with his staff. "The last girl, I didn't want to pay her unemployment, which I would have to do if I fired her. So every day I told her everything she did wrong. And then she quit on her own!" He said happily.
"How long should I plan to stay in Chicago?" I asked this ditzy girl.
"Oh, about a week," she declared.
"Hmm, ok." I knew he needed to do some follow-up assessment post-surgery. Though a week seemed lengthy, I booked it.
Patients fly in all the time to see him and have procedures done, I was told. I would've assumed they'd have some guidance to the process for out-of-towners.

I booked my plane ticket well in advance. The plan was, I'd arrive a day before, check into the motel in Edgewater, close to his office. I'd rest from the plane trip, and the next day, bright and early, I'd report to the hospital.
Everything went wrong.
The summer ticked by as an excruciating countdown to the day I would be liberated into beautiful abs. It was early September 2006 when the day of my deliverance arrived.

His ditzy secretary called a few days before and said, "The doctor wants to go on vacation. Is there any way we can bump this up?"

I explained I already purchased my plane ticket. What did they expect? I was flying in on a Monday and we were doing it on Tuesday.

She reported to the doctor and then called me back. "Is there any way we can do it on Monday? Can you come straight from the airport to the hospital?"

"Well, yes. I suppose so," I said. If someone wished to liberate me one day sooner from this loathsome condition of non-perfect abs, well, I'd just have to let them! Though it wasn't what I planned and wished I could've done it in a more calm frame of mind. Guess the doc's vacation was important.

The weekend before the operation, I started not feeling well. While lying in bed, I had difficulty breathing. I'm not sure what part the stress or anticipation played, but I certainly wasn't planning to not feel well. Coughing, congested, my body became sluggish and awful. A person isn't supposed to have surgery when they're sick.

But there was no fucking way in hell I was not having this surgery! I worked all summer. This is what I had lived for. I'll pretend I'm fine, I reasoned.

The day of the surgery, I fly to Chicago. From plane to taxi and straight to the hospital with my suitcase I go, feeling my chest, phlegmatic and heavy. I was going to smile and say I had no idea what they're talking about if they noticed I wasn't well physically. They could not deny me what I'd worked for.

At the hospital I sign a bunch of papers. On the surgery unit, kindly matronly ladies who work there ask what I'm in for. It's vaguely embarrassing, "Abdominal liposuction," I confess defiantly like one who had been persecuted, burned at the stake. They are discreet and look at me compassionately. Daily, they see the horrors of surgeries: removing tumorous growths! Laparoscopic explorations! Separating conjoined twins! Fierce but necessary mutilations and amputations. But this?

They don't speak their pity for me, though I vaguely sense the reproach.

Dr. Replica is there in the operating room, looking spiffy and happy. "Hey, you got in okay!" He's all smiles and friendliness, in his mask and gown. His jovial way puts me at ease, instantly reminds me why I like him. He makes it all seem fun.

Once I am naked and dressed in the hospital gown, they get started. "Okay, we're going to put this iodine all over you. It's antiseptic so there won't be bacteria in the surgery." I stand there, and get slathered, doused in brown liquid across my torso. I look like some butterball turkey about to be served up for Thanksgiving dinner, knives ripping me apart.

I lay on the stretcher, a mask of oxygen placed on me, the IV propofol drip starts. I'm told, "Count backwards from a hundred."

"A hundred. Ninety-nine. Ninety-eight. Ninety-seven. Ninety-sssssss...." With that, I am out. My head nods down into black unconsciousness.

When I'm under, the doctor makes incisions in my nipples and navel and at a point on my side about four inches out from my nipple. In these incisions, he inserts thin long metal wands that look like knitting needles. With this he sucks out the fat.

I am aware of being shaken, my shoulders jiggled.

"You did great! You did great!" they say.

I'm like, "Wha....? Ok..." Groggy in displacement, they help me into a wheelchair and wheel me into a patient's room.

I wake up later in a tight girdle, a body-hugging suit I'm supposed to wear for a week. A white stocking with a cut-out slot for my genitalia.

"Are you going back to New York tomorrow?" Replica asks me.

"Tomorrow?" I ask astonished. "Your girl told me I needed to stay here for a week."

"Oh...." Awkward silence. Perhaps he's calculating when his vacation can start. "I couldn't draw much fat out of you to put in your ass, though I did some," he says. I am deflated to hear this. We were doing fat grafts, sucking fat from my abs to inject into the globes of my ass. Somehow it didn't register I should've fattened up. I could have pigged out all summer to get meaty had I known it would be helpful.

"Also," he continues, "We ran over time in the emergency room. I never rush surgeries. It takes as long as it takes! So they'll be coming to bill you for the extra time we took in the operating room."

"Ok," I say, out-of-it. I hadn't planned for this. I had a few hundred dollars left in my bank account. Everything had been budgeted. I didn't have a big supply of money laying around for contingencies.

I am in a daze in my recovery room. The billing woman comes and says she'll charge me three hundred for the extra hour in the operating room. I give her my card, not telling her this depletes my budget.

"We'll let you sleep. I'll come check on you in the morning," the doc says.

"Okay..."

I'm hooked up to monitors and an intravenous flow line dispensing morphine into my vein. Every 15 minutes I'm allowed to press a little button to dose myself. It's called patient-controlled analgesia. I stare at the clock in front of the bed. Every 15 minutes on the dot I press the button.

In the morning, Replica reviews my vitals and says, puzzled, "We think you might be getting pneumonia." He brings in an incentive spirometer, a plastic toy-like device used to measure and encourage deep breathing. You inhale and exhale to make the ball inside rise; it's meant to increase lung capacity.

He looks at the untouched food on the table near the bed. "I want you to eat!" He commands. This is the moment I'm coming to realize the striking resemblance this guy, who I thought of as a friend, bears to Count Dracula. Thin with glacial features, he swoops in without warning. As a friend he was jovial to be around; as a doctor his bedside manner is that of a nagging shrew.

I look at the food as if it's a ghastly corpse sprawled before me, reluctantly shovel some into my mouth.

He steps out of the room. 10 minutes later, the nurse is there when I feel the food rising back from within. "I'm gonna puke! Get me a trash can."

She's too late. I overturn the concave plastic lid that covered the food, and into this I wretch. Thick, brown, and goupy like sludge. Anesthesia can produce nausea so maybe it was that combined with the morphine that caused vomiting.

"I ate like you said," I announce sweetly yet hatefully to my new nemesis Doctor Dracula when he's back in the room. My body retaliated against being force-fed. He looks concerned.

"I've ordered you pain medication," he says before I check out. He's thoughtfully arranged for it to be ready at the nearby drive-thru pharmacy.

"Is it going to be there?"

"Yes."

"Ready to pick up? I can just go thru?"

He assures me it will. I take a taxi there.

One of the side effects off morphine is disinhibition. It lets you let yourself go. When the taxi gets to the drive-thru window pharmacy on Broadway, my medication isn't ready and in fact they say it may be a long wait. I'm infuriated. The taxi driver says it may cost a lot, just sitting with the meter running. Since I no longer have excess cash to burn, I pile out of the taxi with my luggage and send the driver on his way. Standing in the parking lot, I scream into the drive-thru window at the pharmacy employees. The morphine had turned me into a deranged person. I prevent other cars from driving up to the window to place their orders. The manager, a burly guy, comes lumbering out to the parking lot like a pissed-off cowboy looking to settle the score.

Frothing at the mouth, I scream a tirade, "*I had surgery and came from the hospital! They said it would be ready and it isn't ready! The taxi left and now I'm here and why isn't this ready? How long does it take! I'm NOT even supposed to lift anything! And I just lifted my suitcases!*" It feels satisfying to scream. In retrospect, I can only think it was the morphine button I pressed every 15 minutes all night long that caused this outburst.

Finally, they get my pills together. I lug my stuff to the curb, hail another cab, ride to the motel.

I check in at the motel, collapse backwards onto the magenta floral bedspread with my clothes still on. I lay with my knees bent, feet on the floor, but my body flat on the bed. The anesthesia is still producing an exhaustion blackout. I pass out completely for about 10 hours in this position with my clothes on, unmoving.

The doc required me to take strong antibiotic pills to avoid the possibility of infection. A side effect of this was that it stripped my intestine of the good bacteria, the natural flora, which helps in digestion. As a result, I had violent diarrhea. I couldn't eat anything for a week. Even drinking water produced seizures of nausea. Splatters of brown liquid ripped out of my ass like a hurricane, the acid excreta scalding my tender hole as it went. The constant wiping and attempting to clean myself made my asshole raw, brutalized; it painfully stung. The diarrhea came after I started the antibiotic and blasted out in regular intervals anytime I dared put anything into my mouth.

Yet I was supposed to remain locked in this tight girdle across my torso for a week? I showered occasionally, but mostly washed myself in the sink as best I could. Showering in the girdle apparatus made it mildew. It took a long time to dry and water didn't remove the shit stains from around my genital region.

The once-white bodysuit became a disgusting shade of light brown, from diarrhea backsplash. The splatters resembled a Jackson Pollock abstract expressionist painting. It was revolting. I felt awful. Alone in a dreary motel room in Chicago.

I made my way to Replica's office-mansion for a follow-up appointment, His mail was strewn on the doorstep outside, and I picked it up. "You're not supposed to lift anything!" he complains, seeing I've reached down to get the mail. He tells me of the possibility of dehiscence, my wounds opening.

When I told Replica of my digestive troubles, he sniffed haughtily, "There are some yogurt pills sometimes people take, to repopulate the flora of their stomach. A place like GNC might have them." He said this with a vague airiness. He didn't understand that I was alone in Chicago and too sick to go on what sounded like a hunting expedition to shop for yogurt pills, which may or may not be effective. Had he told me of this possibility beforehand, I would've come prepared.

He scolded me: I was not allowed to lift anything, as I'd just had sutures and my torso was delicately held together. He didn't understand that I had suitcases to carry. It's not as if I had brought a personal valet with me. I would think, having clients come from out of town on a regular basis, you might make your patients aware of this in advance. Had I known what a struggle everything was going to be afterwards, I could've planned to have my girlfriend Selina come to meet me and hang for a couple days to help take care of me.

I'd booked my plane ticket so that I would have a whole week, but now I realized there was no point in being here a whole week, to have propulsive diarrhea blasting out my ass in a motel room. I decided to take the train back to New York from Chicago. It was cheaper than rebooking my flight. An excruciating 20-hour train journey ensued. We stopped at every tiny town along the way. I was jostled around while I starved, downing antidiarrheal medication all the while and staying close to the bathroom at all times.

Cosmetic surgery made me feel infinitely worse. Physically, after that awful first week, its effects lingered mentally and spiritually. I thought I'd feel better. The day after I had the surgery done, still in a fog, I looked to the sky and thought about my place in the universe. Here I had wanted to be attractive, like the popular guys, yet there was an immediate void. I felt like I'd fallen through the earth. All summer I'd looked forward to it. Now I could see how cosmetic surgery can become compulsive, because once you "fix" one thing, instead of having any sense of resolution, you realize the myriad other things which need fixing too.

"The problem wasn't on the outside," someone said to me later. No amount of tinkering with externals can fix it. The best part was maybe the giddy anticipation, dreaming of how beautiful I'd feel. Sometimes you have to get something to realize you didn't really need it in the first place.

For me, this was the illusion of empowerment. It felt proactive to do something, journey through some cathartic channel for my anxiety. But afterward, I had a soul-shattering epiphany: something bigger was inside me, eating me up. My choice to have surgery was a hopeful one, but there was an ugly debasement to it: caving to the opinions of the others. Even if you win the game, you still lose the game.

There's a beauty to naturalism and the aging process! Now, when I see guys with obvious surgerized bodies, like butt implants, I understand the impulse but also feel a little sad for them that they were so attuned to the perceived opinions of others that they thought they needed this or weren't good enough without it.

After surgery, my abs were flat. When I did crunches, the shadow of a 6-pack was there. The surgery was a success. There were no puckering marks or scar indentations where the fat had been vacuumed out.

When people told me I looked good after that, I was like, "Fuck you bitch! Of course, I look good."
I paid for it in blood and shit, propofol and morphine, vomit and hunger pangs, disillusionment, and spiritual epiphanies.

ST. MARKS HOTEL LOST AND FOUND
Lily Fury

I was wandering aimlessly down St. Marks Street when I found her. She could tell you your dreams if she wasn't so busy destroying her own. Lost and found and lost again. She was beauty and decay and love. She was 26 and in love with her malevolent abusive pimp/boyfriend/baby daddy. I was 18; we were both attempting to escape our damaged pasts with heroin and waiting for saviors that never appeared. I found solace in the streets and the swarms of lost angels, tying off with their own halos. She had her brown hair pulled into a high ponytail, beautiful and rare eyes, one brown and one green that she kept concealed under sunglasses while working that corner in an oversized tee shirt that she had tied up in the front, revealing her sparkling belly button ring and stretch marks from her multiple pregnancies. She's leaning up against the St. Marks Hotel, where many of the street working girls hang around waiting for tricks. She smiles when she sees me approaching, exposing freshly pink gashes in her mouth from newly missing and broken teeth. I suspect her pimp lover but who could know? She would pick up tricks right out front of that hotel, fearlessly and recklessly get into the cars that would circle the blocks and stop for her.

I had just unleashed bile onto the concrete, pupils big and black like the night sky. "Girl, what happened to your teeth?"

She laughs it off with, "It makes sucking dick easier."

We both laugh. Sometimes, all we can do is laugh to fight off the past and present pain that follows us around like a persistent ex-lover. We are orphan blood, Lola and me. When I couldn't find a vein anymore, I had Lola hold up a mirror for me while I shot up in my neck.

I had just gotten back from upstate, where I was working at a strip club for almost a year when I was underage. The manager had never even asked to see my ID, only for me to strip for him in his sleazy office while he jerked off. One night I showed up for my shift only to see the building encased in brilliant flames. I lit a cigarette and watched, mesmerized, as the flames swallowed my club along with my stripper persona, my regulars and my means of survival. I bought a van for $500 the next day that would become my home, a mobile home where I could just up and leave whenever I wanted, and drove to NYC to do a photo-shoot for the porn magazine Barely Legal. Twenty-five hundred dollars that went straight into my veins, and now I was shaking from the sickness.

"I need to borrow some money," I told her.

She said it was slow and she hadn't even been out that long that day, but offered me her rinse, which I gratefully accepted. When I came back outside she was with Maria, an older working girl covered in white trash tattoos. She told the most captivating but obviously fictitious stories, like she once told us she had worked for Heidi Fleiss. She wasn't particularly pretty but she had a self-deprecating humor and an energy about her that drew men to her.

"You turning tricks now, Lily?" I always loved that term because it gives the illusion of magic happening.

"Nah, I'm panhandling near Union Square, but some home bum took my spot today."

"Well I could introduce you to a client if you give me a cut," Maria started.

Lola interrupted, "No, no, no, Lily is too young for this shit." Lola had taken on the role of a protective older sister as soon as she had laid eyes on me, she thought I was a runaway and no amount of persuading would convince her otherwise.

"But not too young to put a needle in her arm or to do porno magazines," Maria huffed. Maria could be your best friend or your worst enemy and that decision was always up to you.

"Five o'clock," Lola said, grabbing my arm protectively. I searched the street just long enough to see his pock marked face. He had been stalking me for months now. Always trying to find me at my most desperate moments and then come up offering money in exchange for sex. He claimed to be a lawyer but his scraggly and greasy appearance told me otherwise, although from what I had learned in my 18 years, I guess anything was possible. The most devious part of his offers was that he didn't want to wear a condom. He fucked the most hopeless and desperate of the street working girls for cheap, getting off on spreading whatever disease we believed he had. He was so cheap with these girls it made me sick. Twenty dollars cheap. So I could see why Maria would be frustrated with me for me not taking him up on his offer of $400 for me. She had previously advised me to just "fade out." If I practiced hard enough, she said, I could separate my brain from my body. All I had to do was lie down. "They cum quick," she said "They could touch. But eventually you wouldn't even really feel." You could become almost lifeless, invisible, on the periphery of consciousness. Your brain blank, your body not your own.

I imagined Maria in some dingy hotel room, naked and in a coma of sorts while a nameless faceless john fucked her. Then I imagined her coming to, collecting her money, and laughing the witch cackle that she laughed on her way out. It was a transformation of sorts and transformation is necessary in this trade of work, whether it's disassociation or giving birth to your stripper alter ego as you rose to the stage in a glittering gold outfit with an artificial smile. Maria made it sound so easy.

Lola's boyfriend Rob emerged seething with rage from around the corner. I detested him, for obvious reasons, but tolerated him for her sake. He started interrogating her about how much money she had made so far. I looked at the "lawyer" man who was still standing across the street as if he was paralyzed in that moment, eyeing me, hungry.

"Rob," I interrupted him while not even looking at him, I was in a world of my own racing thoughts. "Stay here for 20 minutes, please, I'm going upstairs," I said matter-of-factly while I headed across the street to meet the lawyer. Rob was good for protection, if nothing else. Lola's protests died out as Rob silenced her. She crossed her arms and snapped her gum in disapproval.

I went upstairs into a hotel room with the lawyer, and we sat there on the cum and blood stained, faded white sheets covering the bed. Now that he had this illusion of safety he handed me a roll of money. They were all twenties. I counted it.

"You said you were going to give me more than this," I whispered, attempting to sound seductive. He reluctantly handed me another roll. I went to take it from his sweaty, hairy hands but he held on. He looked straight into me with his blank vampire eyes.

"No condom," he said, "And we have to kiss, like girlfriend and boyfriend." Vodka breath and a sly smile sprouted across his face.

I took the money. "Right," I said. He began removing his clothes, revealing a hairy body, lankiness, my repulsion, flappy skin, a dirty penis.

I walked to the bathroom. I felt nauseated. I had left my bag by the door the whole time. I watched him from the mirror until he was completely naked and summoning me to him. "It's a pretty shitty thing to try to fuck your whores with no condom," I said loud and angry as I opened that door and ran as fast as I could away from him.

"Hey, wait a minute bitch, I paid for you," I heard him say on my way out. A slew of vile insults trickled into thin air as I left him behind.

CLASS WHORE
anna saini

Rich people more freely give their money to other rich people. Take, for instance, the W Hotel bar in Times Square, where I survey the crowd, a hive of ego emanating a low-level buzz of cash and vacuous grins. Suits dip into the bar periodically, then pull back circuitously, collide hungrily, pollinate strangers and colleagues, potential mates and business deals. Their speech slacked and slurred with the nectar of alcohol.

It's apparent to me that even the waitresses have more disposable income than I do. They flit around communicating drink orders back to the queen bee at the bar, speckling the scene with their red-soled Louboutins. Foot fetish guys drool for Louboutins; my friend makes a regular weekly income on a guy who gets off on sucking the six-inch heels while she wears them and demeans him. To everyone else the shock of color on the soles acts as a subtle sign of status. For waitresses and hookers, shoes that cost upward of $600 are a business investment. The waitresses here will make that back in tips on a good night here at the W. Or so I think, and that's the point, perception.

Although the place is dimly lit, nothing feels private here. The light flickers on the skin, making the room pulse in a unified thrum. The inlet lamps and the candlelight are intrusive, too illuminating. I feel my stool at the bar is a velvet covered pedestal and the room's eyes bear down on me like spotlights demanding Who are you and why are you here?

I spend several (fourteen) of the last dollars in my moving-to-NY fund on a drink and hope that this trick is not fake. Hope is not the word, because my only option is to walk out of the hotel tomorrow morning three thousand dollars richer, able to pay rent and wanton for an expensive meal or a shopping spree: physical manifestation of an existence I eked out beyond survival.

I am wearing a basic black dress owned since high school. A well-cut designer number I bought at a sample sale. Black leather cradles my slender feet, the back-to-back gold G's of the Gucci logo brand the back of my heels. It's too cold for these shoes in February but they're the only ones that go with my costume. I'm grateful there's no snow on the ground.

I got them from a short-lived sugar-daddy client: an Indian business magnate who wanted exclusive access to me that his wallet couldn't handle. On our first meeting he dropped six bills on my night table and looked at me expecting me to be impressed, grateful even. I just swipe my hand across the tabletop as if I'm removing a film of dust. When the bills fall into the open night table drawer I say thank you and stare at him with a dull glare.

He said he wanted me to be his girlfriend so I forcefully softened my expression, perched my booty on his lap, crossed my long naked legs at the ankle, fondled the stiletto on my cheap high heel and cooed, "Oh honey, I want to be your girlfriend too."

I was annoyed by his mindfuckery already and the session had barely started. Our relationship began with him hemming and hawing as to when he would see me and where we would meet, repeatedly attempting to get me to talk over the phone about what I would and would not do. I firmly reminded him that if he's asking me what sex acts I would trade for money, that's illegal. I wondered for a moment if he was actually an undercover cop, but ruled it out because the police force is cut fairly predictably on race lines in Michigan: Black cops in Detroit and a few of the working class and 'ethnic' inner city suburbs, white cops everywhere else.

I didn't expect that he would actually show up for the appointment he booked with me and I considered his imminent no-show a win-win. I didn't really want to be in the same room with the creep but I need a blatant justification to turn down his money. It's not my business to refuse large sums of cash from folks I find distasteful. I grew up working class poor and most of the time I'm hungry. The oppressive presupposition that he has paid for me, all of me, not just the sex or the hour—it's not enough reason for me to be several hundred dollars poorer, but it made me want to take his money, put him in his place.

He pushed me off his lap. I landed in a tangle of my legs and a wry smirk on the bed beside him. "No, I mean I really want you to be my girlfriend. Tell me your name. I need to know your real name if you're my girlfriend." Seasoned hookers usually prepare a myriad of names for their repertoire: a fake fake name that works like a stage name, a real fake name that you go by on the regular, and a fake real name that you give your clients in situations like these, when they ask one of the most annoying questions that anyone can ask a hooker. I could pull out my fake real name, but instead, I leaned into him and ran the side of my index finger down his cheek from the corner of his eye to his chin in a gesture of theatrical intimacy You already know my name, baby, I'm Asha.

There was a flash of anger in his eyes that he didn't allow to surface on the rest of his face. He kept his expression menacingly cool. He told me he does already know my name; the hotel owner is a friend of his so he called to find out under what name the room is booked. He says my name back to me and it sounds low-class, worthless. I am Indian and he is Indian and he can tell by my last name that I am of a lower caste. Unlike my other Indian clients he rebuffs the dynamic of privilege that puts me on top because I'm a born North American. He took us both back to India, where someone like me should be happy to have someone like him pay a shit ton for my pathetic lower caste pussy.

I used this hotel a lot and now I'll never come back. It's not like I can't tell him to get the fuck out. But I don't. It feels like losing. I have to wait until I'm back on top and that won't happen today since he said he doesn't want to fuck me. He's too busy. He wanted to take me out next time. I agree, fine, shopping.

When we met the next week at the mall me and my friends called the class warfare mall, Somerset Mall, it was my turn to make him feel poverty. I resolved to show this fucking bullshit immigrant his place by taking him where both of us were unwanted refugee vermin.

At Gucci they didn't give a fuck about him and his money. He wandered around the store asking for someone to help his girlfriend find a dress and shoes to wear for him. I felt sorry for him, sorry that he made me do this. I pulled some clothes off the racks: an olive green tank top that costs $650, an army green dress that costs $1200 and the heels that I'm now wearing at the W Hotel bar, the heels that become my upscale hooker staple, $700. I would have bought generic versions of this entire outfit for less than $100 if it was my own money.

From the change room I heard him ask a sales representative What makes these clothes so special, anyway? and I heard the reply: "Do you even know what Gucci is?" As I made my way out of the change-room, several months of rent draped over my crooked forearm on my way to the check-out, He said under his breath, as if this was the secretive thing and I'm his accomplice "You know they have cameras at these cash registers, so I can't dispute the credit card charge."

He took me back to the hotel room; it was a motel room, actually, or an inn to be more specific, the Comfort Inn off of I-97 in Troy. He wanted to meet in a "classier" establishment than the place we originally met, which is fine with me since I would never return to that hotel and this way I didn't have to pay.

When we arrived at the squat orange brick building he at first wanted me to come up to the counter with him, then he got embarrassed and ushered me away to pretend we don't know each other, just two random strangers who walked in to the sullen empty lobby of the Comfort Inn... but not together. I wandered, I checked out the "art," I casually headed down the hallway several meters behind him to the room.

He told me the specialty of the room, it's the honeymoon suite of sorts, there's a jacuzzi. Sure, this seemed like a good idea, hire a hooker and fuck her in a cheap room with a jacuzzi at the Comfort Inn. So much of what clients do with hookers makes sense in their pathetic, horny brains but falls apart under their flimsy, lusty logic in the real world. For instance, jacuzzis are hot and this guy couldn't stay in there for any longer than a few minutes, much less get his dick hard and penetrate me. If there was any chance of that happening, I would've refused, but instead I played dumb like I thought it'd work and then widened my eyes in feigned quizzical wonderment when his member remained a lifeless slab of flesh between my legs. I enjoyed the jets for a few minutes while he sucked on my tits and tried to get an erection. I furrowed my eyebrows in frustration when he blamed the tub for his lack of arousal and tried to beat his now red-brown cock to erection some more. It occurred to me that he intended to fuck me without a condom, which would be offensive if it wasn't so ridiculously out of the question.

Finally I sprung out of the jacuzzi amid his protests, draped a towel around my body and hopped onto the bed in an effortless motion, as if to say "Motherfucker, I am young, you are old, closer to death and I'm not confident about what waits for you in the afterlife."

With much annoying reluctance he lumbered out of the water, wet black hair caked to his chest, legs and back in a fuzzy mold. I realized at that moment that I would not fuck him to completion. Not tonight and not ever. Not even though he paid me all this money, not even though he took me on a several thousand dollar shopping spree, not even for anything. I realized that I wanted to get out of there and never see his ugly face again.

Not because he was dangerous. Clearly, he was dangerous. But that took a back seat to the rush of paying my bills easy for as long as I could hold out with the motherfucker while accumulating all this stuff. I had stayed up all night before our date surfing the website of all the stores in the mall and then each of their catalogs. I made a dream wish-list of a wardrobe based on La Perla and flanked with Louise Vuitton adding an item for each imagined subsequent shopping spree date.

He was irritating, gross, and mean-spirited but one or a combination of these terms could be used to describe many of my clientele. He offered to make arrangements to redecorate my home, put me up in an apartment and buy me a car and I believed his offers to be genuine. He told me that if I would just give him my address then he would ship the furniture there, he would even send a re-decorator. "Just be honest with me though, do you live in a whorehouse? Is it a brothel? Tell the truth!"

"No it's not a brothel (idiot), I live in a house and I don't want you to ever know where I live."

I made my moves to get out of there. He was mad and I had no reassurance that he wouldn't hit me but I made sure to pluck each shopping bag lovingly off of the floor of our room at the Comfort Inn.

I got to the door and stopped as he slung insults at my back, I slipped off my sandals and threw them in one of the bags, opened up my shoebox and slipped on my new Gucci's for the first time. In the shit-storm of his curses I walked out of there a few inches taller in the shoes and posture of a working-class Cinderella.

DESOLATION ROW
Rita Rachaels

This poem is for all your lights out –
every single one.
I will never hold a candle again
to anyone's face and believe
that what I'm seeing is true
never never again.
I will never trust
the voyage of water lilies
as they meander
down spring time creeks and streams
never never again.
I will never give
more than a passing ear
to any of your "I Love Yous"
cloaked in poetry,
concealing with a thin veneer
the emptiness of your declarations.
But more than anything else
I will not expect you
to keep your appointment
at my grave
To remember all I gave you again
and again and yet even more.
No I will pass by your mind
like a falling leaf
and by your heart
nothing more than a grain of sand.

COME CLEAN
Rei

My joke was that being into discipline meant you were the
Republican party of the kink scene. One could be a member of
the Grand Old Party anyway, but it wasn't your political
conviction that got you the label. This conservatism was ready to
burst at the seams of freshly pressed button down shirts, while
holding modestly cut skirts below the knees. My own clients'
cocks were invisible, their erections hidden by carefully cut
oxford button-downs and boxer shorts. If there was any
evidence of arousal—tenting, a pool of precum connecting their
genitals to the floor—it went ignored.

      This stood in stark contrast to our seemingly more
freewheeling cousins who were into sadism and masochism. If
leather- and latex-clad dominatrices held an air of sex about
them, disciplinarians firmly reminded you that there was none to
be had here. We managed to cut the sex out of the act of pulling
our clients' pants down to spank them. Never once did it occur
to us to have them take off their shirts. This was not sex, this was
not sexual.

      Discipline was safe, I supposed. At least, I went into
because it felt safe. My first six months working as a professional
submissive found me in unreasonable amounts of pain nearly
daily. My clients' punishments for me ran the gamut from stupid
to unconscionable. There was Paul, whose mission was to
stretch my labia to my knees, and who whipped me if the
dreaded hemostat clamps slid off when I got wet. Joe would lay
me on my back and threaten to violently paddle my thighs, just

because he thought I looked cute when I squeezed my eyes to brace for the landing. My employer was in on it as well, stopping just short of calling me a pussy for not being able to take a breast caning at 2am.

Once I left there I started working with Lynne, who rented from the place I worked at, but left along with me. Lynne was different. She didn't call herself a dominatrix and never once cursed in session. Her clients were working-class guys who feared and respected her.

She taught me how to give a ten-minute hand-spanking without flinching or losing my breath. She showed me the marks that leather could leave and the blisters that could be raised by wood paddles. Working in my underwear would no longer be acceptable, as my clients were going to be slightly stripped down and I needed to be more clothed than they. They'd never see me naked. If they were really into this end of things, I'd never see them naked, either.

We ended up working in Central New Jersey, out of a motel in the middle of nowhere.

"I can fuck my wife anytime," one of my earliest clients confessed. "This, this is what I come here for."

He'd punctuate it by turning away from me and keeping a careful hand over his burgeoning erection, bent over the creaking motel bed. Though I knew being struck made him painfully hard, he never asked to finish off in front of me. He kept himself hidden away between every change in position— never exposing himself to me.

Confessions from other clients would reveal more than just a desire to be faithful. Some of it was age—with my mostly older clients only getting to act on this long after they were conditioned to a life of keeping it hidden. Others felt genuine shame and needed to atone for something specific and sex would just kill the fantasy.

So I wrapped myself in crisp blouses and tan stockings. I went from wearing spiked heels to sensible flats. I was their mother, their aunt, their neighbor or the mean girl next door. I developed a love for leather straps and ended up making a short, doubled leather belt my signature implement. I made maps out of my clients' asses—their cheeks were split into quadrants of prolonged and unbearable pain.

I went a year without being struck. I was untouched and I adored every second of it.

Lynne eventually moved out of Jersey, giving me little incentive to continue seeing clients at that motel. I was living in Northern New Jersey, just outside of Manhattan at the time, and my commute to the motel involved three trains and a lot of patience. I was missing New York and it was easier to cross the Hudson River for work.

I'd learn that renting a space in New York meant renting from a dungeon, and that no house had a domestic setting like I was used to in the hotels. I took a lot of comfort in being able to lay my clients face down on a bed, or bend them over a chair. Every available dungeon room felt cramped with their ubiquitous St. Andrew's crosses, and leather massage tables. There was no place that could evoke the safety of someone's private home.

After a bit of trial and error, I landed at a place in Midtown. Though I was unhappy at the prospect of not having the comfort of home furniture, I could at least feel a sense of security in the owner, William's, means of doing business.

"You don't give 'extras' right?" His accent was Old New York on four cups of coffee.

"No, really. All I do is domestic discipline." I insisted. "I don't even think these guys have dicks, you know? I never see them naked."

"Good, because I have rules here, alright? None of my girls get naked, so neither do you. No blowjobs, no hand jobs, no nothing, alright?"

I found further comfort in the fact that William was also a complete germaphobe. He didn't shake hands and needed an exact notation of which implements you used when you were in the room. Use meant any you brushed your fingers against, which his wife, who answered the phones, had a knack for figuring out on the spot. If one crop shifted out of place, she would know, and hastily tell you to wipe it down, lest you lose your rental privileges.

The space was close enough to walk to from Port Authority, greatly simplifying my commute. It had three available rooms and a bathroom, if needed. The best room was the red-walled room at the end of the hall, opposite the bathroom. Despite being crowded by a massage table, spanking bench and cross, it was the largest room and had the best working air conditioner. It was furthest from the reception area, nearly unlit by the hall light, minimizing the risk of accidental walk-ins, should other clients be wandering the floor for any reason.

I was as safe as I could be, hoping my clients would politely ignore the glass case of nipple clamps in the corner of the best room.

I was at there for about a month when Benjamin found one of my ads and took it as an opportunity to constantly text rather than make a single call or email. The messages were nearly indecipherable, with the number 2 used to replace the word 'to' at every opportunity and managing to spell ma'am in five different ways. He wanted to be beaten with my leather straps, only, and with no warm-up.

No OTK. Nothing w/ yr hand. Just the strap.

He kept insisting that I meet him in south Brooklyn, close to Sheepshead Bay, where he lived. As a former resident of Bay Ridge, his location endeared me, but his persistence threatened to kill the appeal. Like many clients, he assumed I had all my implements at hand and could just get up and go. As if I carried my leather straps with me when I did things like run to the supermarket and was willing to drop everything to spank him. After weeks of asking me to come to Brooklyn in sixty minutes or less. he finally committed to a night in Manhattan.

I had to wait for my all clients on the street outside, as it was easier to walk them up and safer than revealing the floor number right away. It was late enough that I could be certain the sole 5'9 body walking toward me was him. He had brown, close-cropped hair and pale blue eyes, with plush lips to round out his young face. His ADIDAS tracksuit matched the backpack over his shoulder. His sneakers were extraordinarily clean.

"Benjamin?" I asked sharply, once he got close.

"Yes, ma'am?" Eastern European accent, light enough to indicate that he immigrated to Sheepshead Bay when he was young, but not young enough to shed his roots. He smiled and looked down at his shoes before looking up at me again, like a teenage boy.

"How old are you?" I demanded.

"I'm 28," he said, looking at his shoes again. Though he looked like he was over 20, his boyish looks threw me on a curve. He was a kid in comparison to the suburban fifty-somethings I had taken over my lap. The flush across his cheeks was almost comical, melting the hard front I had been building.

"What, you want to see?" he asked. He fished into the pocket of his tracksuit and pulled out his wallet. A New York State ID with a birth year of 1979 was held to my face.

Good enough.

I ushered him upstairs, showing William's wife that I had implements of my own in my bag and nothing would be out of place. I paid the rental fee, led him to the red room, and then Benjamin and I were alone, finally.

He didn't wait for me to instruct him to undress, or for me to walk over and undress him. He settled his backpack down on the massage table against the window and toed off his sneakers. I watched as he slid out of his track pants and unzipped his windbreaker, folding them and securing them under the bag.

He stretched his muscled arms above his head, tightening the ribbed white undershirt over his chest. Fine Chinese Pinyin was tattooed into his biceps, over matching tigers cascading to his elbows. His plaid boxers fell delicately over a well-muscled ass. He still had his socks on.

He pulled his undershirt over his head. The boxers slipped off as if this were quite routine. He folded them both, along with the tracksuit. He turned, stood straight and looked at me directly; his flaccid cock lay against his left thigh, the head ending almost midway.

A squeak escaped my throat and his eyes shot down to the floor again. There was his cock, in plain sight. Though he was looking in its general direction, he made no move to cover himself with his hands.

I didn't want to believe that the year of safety also meant a year of avoidance, but one look at his slightly flushed head started to bring the thought to light. When was the last time I saw a full-on cock? What the hell was I supposed to do with one? I hadn't had heterosexual sex in at least a year a half, and the mechanics of fucking would be of no help here.

I thought back to all the straight things I did before all cock was banished. My ex's cock barely fitting between my legs and his insistence on taking my ass. The rebound fucks with the boy with the frenum piercing and how my passionate screams kicked off that sunny Brooklyn Sunday morning. The one time I ever really made love and didn't feel like a sap afterwards. Even the teenage backseat fingering in the parking lots of Jersey goth clubs came back to me, in phallic waves.

My thoughts were racing; I dug my fingernails into my palms to bring myself back. This was not sex and this was not sexual, no matter how attractive the body in front of me was.

"Just start," he said. He turned and walked over to the large St. Andrew's cross nailed to the wall. He faced it, placed his hands on the upper crossbeams, and pushed his ass out toward me.

The trip down memory lane had made me forget where my implements were, exactly. I scuttled under the massage table, looking for my longest strap, palms sweating as its absence seemed apparent. After what felt like an eternity, I found it and the rest of my things.

I made a tight grip over the handle and stood a little closer. The strap was about 20 inches long and five wide. This was unusual for me as wielding anything over 17 inches meant that my strikes wouldn't be consistent, but I was scrambling for distance.

It took a year to get the math right- I was 4'10, so the implement couldn't be too close to my 26-inch sleeve length because my right arm was stronger than my left and cancel the whole thing out.

It was junk science, really. I didn't understand the physics behind what I was doing. All I knew is that a year of issuing discipline meant 17 was the magic number if I wanted to do this right. 20 meant I was throwing it out the window.

"Are you going to start?" he asked, plainly.

"What are you, fucking rushing me?" I said through my teeth.

"No, you're just being so quiet."

"I'll show you quiet."

I reached back and landed an even blow across both cheeks. The math had failed and I had triumphed in the face of arousal. He was met with four more perfect landings, the proof in the red lines surfacing on his rear.

His response was a single cough. I had been celebrating alone.

Not to be deterred, I reached back and gave it a bit more force. My aim did slip at points, landing a bit too close to the outer portions of his thighs and a hair below the seam where his ass ended. After 25 strikes, I was running out of breath. He simply leaned his head into his right shoulder and gave a wavering, but tired-sounding sigh.

"Am I boring you?" I asked angrily.

"No. You just have to keep going."

It wasn't unusual for a client to ask me to skip the warm up and go directly to being strapped. Some wanted it to just be over already—skip straight to the quick cry and tell me how sorry they were. These sessions were usually short as any sudden blow to the rear kicked up their 'fight or flight' reactions, breaking any confidence they had walking in. Benjamin was having none of that. Benjamin was going to make me work for it

I chucked the strap aside and went for my shorter belt. This meant I had to stand a little closer.

I smelled his sweat first, and then saw it forming on his back and shoulders. The back of his head was pebbled with salty beads. His breathing remained even.

Sweat wasn't new. Everyone sweat. But everyone didn't stand stock still while they did it. He was supposed to be asking how much longer he had to go and giving me looks over his shoulder at what was coming next.

He wasn't supposed to smell this good, either.

"Are we starting?"

"Stop talking." I stood perpendicular to him, giving me full view of his side. I could see his cock, but he had turned his hips away, just enough to show me more of his rear. I had to make sure the flat of the leather would hit, rather than the tip. If he got the full slap of it, perhaps he would at least try to wriggle out of the way.

I landed across his ass and pulled back a few steps to land on the outside of his thighs again, moving back and forth between his full rear and more sensitive thigh area. I'd let a stray blow land to the tops of his thighs to see if he'd at least flinch, but to no avail. His skin had started to puff up, his blood rushing to the surface.

I remained zeroed in on his ass as my arm started cramping. There was a little reverb as the tip of the strap hit my forearm, forming an angry mark. My shoulder was locking up and I myself was starting to sweat. My white blouse stuck to my chest and started to become untucked. I lost count of the number of strikes and I had stopped caring. All I knew was that my empire of control was crumbling and I was losing ground.

My breathing became a bit more uneven and I blindly reached out for something to hold on to. Being so focused on his thick legs and abraded skin, I thought I was going to be pressing my hands into red concrete. My free hand instead landed on the slick of a thick arm. He gave a sharp grunt—the first noise I had heard beyond my strikes and failing breath. I was so taken by surprise that I dropped the belt and pulled back.

Benjamin straightened himself out, giving me a straight side view. His cock was swollen—the plump head mere centimeters from the cross joint.

"Oh fuck," he gasped.

"Aw fuck," I wailed.

His breathing was finally labored. He pressed his head to a patch of wall above the cross and canted his hips. Rivulets of sweat trickled slowly down his back. Heavier drops made it down the curve of his ass to meet stray red cuts. He sucked his breath in through his teeth.

I wiped my sweaty palms on my skirt and pulled out whatever was secured to the waistband. I felt sticky. My thighs were slick with my own sweat and my panties had ridden up-secured to my crotch by a familiar wetness. Whatever I thought I had killed had come back in the form of a hardbody with a delicious amount of pain tolerance. The room reeked of a crime about to be committed- my blood pounded in my ears.

"You can use your hands." he mumbled, pressing his face into his shoulder.

I didn't want to use my hands. I wanted to use my mouth and my tongue and the suction I knew I could make with my cheeks. I wanted to bury his cock down my throat, my palms splayed over my handiwork for balance.

"I don't do extras."

"Please?" He canted his hips again. His head was nudging the crux. William's wife could probably smell ejaculate stains.

I unbuttoned my shirt and let it fall to the floor. I got in close behind him, enough to count the short hairs on the back of his neck. Grabbing one ass cheek with my left, I dug my fingernails into his abraded flesh. He cried out and tried to pull away, but my nails held firm. I pressed my breasts into his back, leaning in for a little balance. My forehead met his spine, our sweat co-mingled. I slid my right hand around his waist and curled it around the base of his cock.

Fuck starched shirts and nagging aunties. Fuck pretending no one ever got off.

Fuck the empire.

Fuck it all.

I had a clumsy start. My hand was too dry, stuttering my strokes. His ass kept bumping out against my pubic bone, throwing me off balance. He gently pried my hand away. I heard him spit and felt him take my wrist again. We started over.

When I first started working, I felt as if I were permanently covered in fluid. I was the only one in the house who wasn't on the pill, so I bled and ruined my panties. Everyone had piss clients and great aim, and I could never keep the spray from making it back onto my own thighs. Enemas misfired. Canes cut me too deeply. My world was viscous, red and salty. It was impossible to feel clean.

Benjamin's body was blood and salt now. Though I was slick with him, I wouldn't be sullied by the act. I'd make him come and it wouldn't ruin me. Through blood and salt and come— through him—I'd be clean.

The spit was starting to dry out, but by his shortness of breath, I knew he was close. I squeezed my eyes shut, rendering the world red. With one breath, I dug my nails into his ass again. With one final yell, he jerked forward. His back and rose and fell. His cock pulsed in my hand.

I peeled myself off his back. The cool of the room started to dry my skin. I didn't make any move to wipe myself down. I decided to wait for the delicate shell to form across my face and breasts.

Benjamin turned and walked off to gather up his clothes. A telltale cloudy stain slid quietly down the cross beam to the wall.

Lifting my leg carefully, I wiped it off with the bottom of my sensible flats.

SHAME ON ME
Nicolette Dixon

I think about stripping all the time. Even though it has been
almost three years since I last flashed my ass for cash, the
lessons learned in my on again off again time in strip clubs infest
my daily life. The memories from my stripper past are always
waiting for me, like a surprise twenty in my coat pocket or a
moldy lemon in the back of the fridge drawer.

When I look back, the days and the nights in the
windowless red tinged oases bleed together in a flow of cherry
lip gloss, sweaty skin, crowded dressing rooms, and crumpled
dollar bills. But strong emotions always make one memory turn
up a little brighter than the rest, supported by the rush of
neurochemicals. The flow is interrupted by the pop of a moment
that has the heat of emotion behind it. Shame is one of those
emotions that stain the gallery walls of your memory. I remember
the first time I felt shame in a strip club. Roughly a decade ago,
early in my career, but not right away. It came with a rush from
one specific exchange.

I held my client's hand as I led him into the lap dance
booth. I am the corrupter, leading the uninitiated into the
sanctioned space. This is my specialty, the young ones with
puppy eyes and pimples. They are clean cut and sneaker shod. I
know the old men have more money, but at 19 I'm a baby myself
and I balk at the inscription of so many years on an old man's
skin. I worry if I get too close I will smell his mortality.

Now, I ponder: "Where is it that shame comes from?" It comes from comparing yourself to others and finding a distance, being severed from the awareness that other people feel like you do, and weirdness is ubiquitous. Shame comes from secrets, the ones we keep and the ones that are kept from us. Back then, I thought shame was something I felt when I did something wrong, when I was alone in my unconscionable actions.

Alienated by aging, I went for the fresh faced youths. And I was lucky because in my seaside military town there were a lot of them with expendable cash craving the feminine touch. They came in clusters, new ones all the time. They got paid via direct deposit at midnight on Fridays, so on Thursday from 9:00-11:45 they played pool and drank coca-cola.

This particular Thursday, I've been shooting pool at the back table with a trio of sailors. I'm no good at the game, but it gives me a chance to bend over a lot, and my seductive poses have paid off.

Now I have learned that shame has an antidote: revelation. I have eased other people's shame with my ready admittance to living with herpes. A poem I heard once about masturbating by humping a pillow erased years of the shame I felt about that act. I know that talking about the things we are told not to talk about is hard, but if we look at our effort as a gift to another, perhaps it will become a little easier. Someone could have saved my 19 year old self a lot of shame if they warned me that it's possible a guy will cum in a lap dance, and that both of you will be unprepared for it.

Even in my early days, I have rituals. I hold his hand while I lead him to the booth, I look over my shoulder about half way there. I swoop my hand through the beaded curtain when we arrive (love the rainstorm sound of the movement and the texture of the smooth globes of wood against my fingers), then pivot in my 8 inch heels as I clear the entry way for him.

Tonight I offer passage to Sean. My sailor is sturdy and stout in loose fitting jeans and a polo shirt. He's nervous, but that doesn't stop him from commenting on how soft my skin is, even though all the signs say no touching.

It's all grinding. This is what I didn't know before I started stripping. This is what I always assume the other girls know how to avoid. What are the secrets to giving a lap dance with more dance than lap? Most of my lap dances resemble the Friday night first date dry hump fests I had in high school more than anything out of Flash Dance or Showgirls. What I didn't know then is that this isn't unique to me.

More ritual ensues once our song begins. I face him, brief eye contact, lean my face close to his neck, my breasts touch his face before I slide down his body to find my head in his lap. The length of a dance varies depending on the client. Each song is twenty dollars, and at the end of a song I coo into his ear, "Would you like another?" My average time with a guy is four or five songs, each song cut down to two minutes by the club. Unconscious choreography gets me through the first song, maybe two, but then it's all grinding.

Evacuate. Expel. Shoot. Surge. Squirt. Swell. Spray. Pump. Purge. Plaster. Drain. Dislodge. Dislocated agents of creation.

Sticky spooge leaks through his big jeans all over my legs.

I am mortified. I have no idea what to do. I'm not sure it has actually happened. I hadn't imagined that would ever happen. No one even told me this might happen. Uh-oh. It definitely happened. What if someone saw me walking out and could tell-what if they saw the sheen on my thighs, the stain on his big jeans?

I act like nothing has happened as we make our way to the ATM, where he withdraws a quarter of his paycheck, then to the cash register where he pays the club for their services and me for mine. He tips well, an extra $50 on top of the standard fee. It doesn't feel like enough. Not necessarily that the money doesn't compensate for the act, but that it doesn't compensate for my silence, bewilderment, or disillusion. I was so unprepared for this: my first time feeling shame in a strip club.

I didn't talk about it to anyone that night. I snuck into the dressing room and wiped my whole body down with baby wipes before returning to work. Gradually, I let the story leak out to girls I felt comfortable with, but no one would admit to a similar occurrence. Mostly I talked to the other new-ish girls, and they looked as shocked as I had been when it happened.

One day Bonita heard about it. Bonita had been dancing for at least 20 years. She was in her 40s but still strikingly attractive. She had the most unusual stage sets I'd ever seen. She didn't dance or move much at all. She took all her clothes off before she started, then went through a series of artistic frozen poses, about six poses for each set. She would tell anyone anything and didn't seem to have much to hide. Bonita finally set me at peace.

"Oh that happens sometimes to everyone," she said.

"Anyone who says different is lying," she said.

"How much extra did you charge him," she said.

"You could always keep a couple baby wipes in your purse just in case."

I felt better. Bonita was kooky, she held eye contact a little too long, she sometimes didn't wear shoes. But from what I could see, she had nothing to be ashamed of. And she had been accidentally cum on in a lap dance. Looking back, it's a valuable lesson learned. If we were all just a little more honest, maybe we'd all feel a whole lot better about the very human mishaps that we slip on from time to time.

I REMEMBER MARKET STREET CINEMA
Hima B.

I remember visiting Paula at the Market Street Cinema months before I ever work there, never once suspecting that I'd join her as one of many semi-naked women writhing on unknown men's laps for $5 a song. I frequently visit Paula at this strip club but it's only later, when I work there, that I notice how sketchy Market is between 6th and 7th Streets. I stand in the lobby and avert my eyes from the pictures of porn stars headlining at the club, with each boob bigger than their heads. I've come to offer Paula my gift of homemade spicy vegetables, tofu and vermicelli, and bring her favorite guava juice. One day, Paula asks if I want to see the inside of the club. The manager OKs it. After my eyes adjust to the darkness, I see it's a movie theater, except where the screen should be are tacky paintings of naked ladies and the catwalk is a non-stop ant crawl of women getting naked over the course of a three song set. My eyes trace every move Paula makes and I hope they burn her customer as she sits on his lap and rides him after collecting her tip. I feel betrayed. Later I corner her, "How is what you do with customers different than what you do with me?" Paula silences me with a soft kiss. Why is my first adult romance with a girl a Brazilian stripper?

I remember Christmas 1992 at Paula's. I'm confused by her ability to live and work with Pat, her recent ex-girlfriend who introduced her to the world of stripping and photography. I'm down to my last $62. I confess I'm scraping by with loans for house rent from one of my sisters, since being laid off from my telemarketing job. Pat proposes I work with them for a month. "Play up the Indian thing—put on an accent, wear a dot, strip in a sari, and dance to Bollywood songs!" Pat suggests. But even more, I'm afraid I'll burn in Hindu hell if I even consider it. She entices me with promises that I can comfortably quit after a month with a nice savings. I'm sick of being poor but more sickened to ask family for more money.

I remember begging my gay ex-roommate Russ to train me to dance so I won't make a fool of myself during my audition. In his Church Street apartment, he swishes his shoulder-length blonde locks side to side like a super model as his lean body struts to Stevie Wonder in flawless, organic choreography while my attempts to mimic Russ are that of a desperate copycat. We brainstorm on stripper names. "Sabrina" he exclaims, recalling Samantha's wicked twin cousin from "Bewitched." I modify it to "Surina" thinking it sounds just a little bit Indian. Years later, I learn it's a Sanskrit name meaning "Goddess." But years before that revelation, I come across a lesbian Muslim activist with that moniker but I'm too embarrassed to tell her that I use it as my stage name.

I remember post-Christmas 1992. Ziad sits at the manager/DJ booth in the strip club lobby while below him are Polaroids of girls working that shift. Paula introduces me as a friend in need of job. I'm disappointed it's not as her girlfriend. "Eleven am show, honey," he mutters with a smile, meaning that I am hired. Later I discover there's no audition process at this club, no employment paperwork to fill out. You just show up, the manager quickly assesses your physique with his x-ray vision and scribbles your name onto the dance rotation. Later I learn that most of management are Lebanese or from other parts of the Middle East. I imagine Ziad eating falafel with his young daughter and wonder how he explains his job managing naked American girls to his unconditionally accepting, silent wife.

I remember the first time I strip. Eleven am show. Five faces peer back at me as I look out into a dark theatre. I forget to smile as I'm caught up in a naked whirlpool. At the end of my set, I scrape some singles off the stage and stand exhausted with conflicting feelings of anger and shame. Should I be happy there's not more guys in the room to see my nakedness? I want to scream as I look at $3 I've earned for taking off all my clothes but all that comes out is a whimper of strained breathing because I'm out of shape. I get dressed behind stage and re-enter the audience clothed. A young Chinese man with a severe cleft palate greets me and waves his $5 bill for a lapdance. I'm horrified that he is who I attract as I take my place on his lap and his hands grip my hips and rock me over his boner. Later during my shift, a different manager leads me down to a cavernous basement office where I can easily disappear with no trace. He takes a Polaroid of me seated on a plush chair. My image is added to those of others on the lobby billboard alerting customers that I, too, now work there. It's framed with my stage name officiating my birth as a sex worker.

I remember that after my first week of stripping I make $1000, after working only 24 hours. Before this, it took me nearly one month of working full time in my telemarketing job where I would plead with San Francisco voters to pass a proposition to make China Basin a commercial zone. I decide to keep stripping, and one month turns into seven years.

I remember 1993 when the mandatory "uniform" at Market Street Cinema are panties underneath a one-piece bodysuit. Although the city is the epicenter of HIV/AIDS, some San Franciscans remain ignorant about safer sex, and Market Street management is amongst the population of uninformed. Some girls wear sheer, netted, or lacy one-pieces but rarely opaque unless they are neon. Customers aren't allowed to touch your crotch or tits and management monitors them and warns those who cross the line. At some point, a girl wears a bra and panties connected by shoelaces on both hips. Others follow this fashion faux pas. Then the trend shifts to a bra and one thong. In two years, as management increasingly siphons money from us, how we dress no longer matters. We are now indoor street walkers unified in desperation to hand over $200 to $300 stage fees to management. Nearly a decade later, strippers at Mitchell Brother(s) walk around completely naked and advertise their wares, foregoing the need for customers to imagine anything. Their private booths are fully stocked with condoms and lube. At the Market Street Cinema, women discretely hide their own condoms in purses while other "strippers" in denial that they're prostitutes have unsafe sex to make their pimp fees.

I remember Jaguar, a 16 year-old white stoner who dances to Cypress Hill and passes for a girl in her early 20s. She's run away from home and now supports herself stripping. I want to baby her, but the reality is that she's far more street savvy than my then 26 year-old self. You'd be straight-up stupid to mess with Jaguar without 26 other strippers jumping to her rescue if she failed to slice you herself. Nonetheless, it breaks my heart that a teen who should be struggling late night with homework and high school romance is instead grinding on men old enough to be an older brother, dad, or grandfather. If customers knew she was 16, would they get still lap dances from her?

I remember the initial shock I feel as I visually survey the women working at Market Street Cinema, where all of Playboy's standards of beauty disintegrate. Jenna Tell, a pear-shaped white junkie, says she's saving for a tit job. Anna, a wrinkled 40-plus-year-old artist with a sexy husky German accent, is in the Osho cult with the club's toned Brazilian strippers. This is the only club where women with saggy tits, bellies unable to hide cesarean scars ,or cellulite can work without a house mom telling them to lose weight, or that they've already filled their Black quota. It's a strange moment of feminism as sex work liberates those of us who've heard that we're not sexy or acceptable by providing us with customers who pay for our company. If 60-year-old Cassie from Chez Paree can make it in the sex industry, then any woman can and live a comfortable life. Later, when the club's $200 commission system kicks in, many of us feel stuck at this club because we know we won't get hired in the "gentlemen's" clubs which perpetuate the white Barbie capitalist narrative of success and beauty.

I remember how quickly the scent of soap and cheap perfume dissipates and is replaced by the sex funk of men lap danced over countless cigarettes as their muskiness permeates through my panties and melanized epidermis. My elbow-length black gloves are a farce at elegance and primarily serve as barriers between me and the sexual lepers for whom this venue has become the focal point of their sex lives. When it dawns on me that stripping is my sex life also, I indiscriminately date women and my bisexuality evaporates into lesbianism. I don't always lap dance. Sometimes, I enjoy conversation with customers about art, pop culture, and life. If they were more attractive, these customers could easily date cool women and there'd be no need for me or this club. But their guts, or age, or social awkwardness prevents them from making those connections. I make peace that if some men need to pay for sexual or human contact, thank God there's women like me who supply it and get paid for it.

I remember a teenage Jade Blue when she first arrives to Market Street Cinema. One night in the dressing room, she shares a picture of knee-length five-inch heeled black boots with spikes and buckles the whole length and asks if they're worth $300. Econo 'ho that I am, I can't justify the price tag—especially not for work. The next day she sports them proudly on stage. I might be in the middle of a lap dance or downstairs in the dressing room but as soon as I hear Einstürzende Neubauten, I gravitate to the stage for Jade's riveting performances.

My jaw hangs in disbelief and deep respect for her craft, which is improvised genius and antithesis to the standard stripper show except for the fact that she happens to be naked. Jade plays with fire, slathers paint on her toned androgynous body, & binds it in tape. Performing oozes out of Jade's DNA and stripping merely offers her a stage and audience to rehearse and hone her skills for what will later become her signature acts. She struggles landing customers, which baffles me, so I pull her aside and suggest that she tone down her goth/punk/dyke exterior to approximate a "nice" Japanese girl. Instead, I am a joke.

"I can't," Jade cuts me off, "it's not me."

I retort, "But what's the point of being here if you're not making money?" Money doesn't motivate Jade like it does the rest of us. "Customers just want tits, ass, pussy. Your art is lost on them," I plead.

When Jade performs the same numbers in dyke or art venues, she instantly rises to super star fame as a contortionist extraordinaire. After Market Street, Jade supplements her income as a dominatrix, porn star, and prostitute. She is inches from getting a big break when Cirque Du Soleil wants her. Because she is undocumented and used a dead person's identity, the government hunts her down but she flees the country in time. Somewhere in the heart of the Amazon, Jade continues her art.

I remember this Black corporate guy who finds me a novelty because I'm the first Indian stripper he's ever met. "You're like a business woman," he complains when I ask him for another tip and ruin his Kama Sutra fantasies. "You're a robot," he concludes as he tells me that I need to loosen up.

I ask, "How many Indian robots do you know who lap dance?" I discover that drinking helps take the edge off dealing with customers like him, and I become a little nicer when my buzz kicks in. He continues to come in for me and tells me he wants to get to know me outside the club—as a person—of course! I relent after he nags me for months and bill him $200 to go out to dinner. We dine together a few times but he constantly steers our conversation to visiting a nearby hot tub. The final time I refuse, he reneges on paying me for our dinner date. That night I dream we're at the hot tubs and I slip a tab of acid in his drink and watch as he quietly trips thinking he's going insane and leave him.

I remember March 1993 when the club announces that we must now pay them $5 a shift to work. Five dollars seems insignificant, but the only other strippers who feel it's unfair are the other queer women, and I'm convinced this is because we're already over men telling us how we're supposed to use our bodies. We whisper revolution as we pass out copies of our zine Queens of the Tenderloin to enlist support for a strike. One article calculates the money the club makes off of us and includes how much management "saves" not paying us wages. Another article offers remedies for yeast infections. Devora, a UC Berkeley undergrad alumna who becomes a good friend tells me, "Stop being a cheap bitch and pay them. We don't even pay taxes!" A couple of months later, the stage fee is raised to $25. In 1995, we're forced to pay $200 to work half a shift.

I remember spotting my former manager Brian from Oh La La Café on Market near 2nd Street in the audience of Market Street Cinema. Seeing his painfully thin, bony frame reminds me of Brian's controlling behavior and OCD about lining up the almond croissants and bear claws in the glass display case in a particular way. Paralyzed at the back of the club, I watch other dancers make their money and pray he'll leave before my stage show. After 15 minutes of watching him reject various dancers and imagining his type, I'm disheartened to see Brian settle comfortably into his seat. I drown my embarrassment and make my rounds through the rows of customers till I stand before him. I'd usually ask, "Would you like some company?" but now it feels inappropriate, creepy, and weirdly incestuous to offer a lap dance. As he tells me he's still managing Oh La La, I feel us both silently judge the other's work choices. As I walk away, I'm secretly delighted that I make more money stripping one shift than I did in one 40 hour work week grinding coffee at 5 am and filling cappuccino and latte orders for Financial District corporate drones.

I remember arguing with a Black customer who insists that I'm not Asian after demanding to know what I am. "India is on the Asian subcontinent. Take a geography class," I tell him as I walk away.

I remember coming to work one day and Mike the manager tells me that Habib, the owner, wants to see me. I'm led to the basement office where an old man with a Middle Eastern accent asks me why I'm not happy at working at his club. Mike stands off to the side and takes out a gun and lets off several rounds onto a wall across the room. They've created a private firing range down here and while I'm terrified, I hope they pass the gun to me and let me at it, which is a faint reality. "I'm happy here," I lie, "I don't have any problems."

Habib mildly asks, "Then why are you creating problems?" I realize that he's figured out that I'm one of the girls behind the Queens of the Tenderloin newsletter. "Well, come see me if you have any problems," he gently says and dismisses me.

I remember New Year's 1995 at Market Street Cinema. Management unveils the themed back rooms, now call us employees, pay us minimum wages, and switch the $25 stage fee to a $200 commission system. There's a shower room and the Bangkok Live stage. Another room shows non-stop porn on the front wall while the back wall is a series of cubicles resembling open telephone booths. Yet another room triangulates with seating along the left wall and gets progressively pitch black the further in you go. Girls scramble to offer hand-jobs and blow-jobs to pay their pimps' fees at the end of the shift. One obese white girl has three customers lined up for her hand-jobs. My regular Mike, a fat jovial guy, comes in to see me and is stunned with the transformation. He wants to "only" touch my tits but I recoil at his touch and hope he doesn't notice the white girl sitting immediately to my left who is letting an Asian customer go down on her. But Mike notices them—he'd have to be blind not to! Either I've gotta give up something or else his money will walk to the seat next to me so I let him play with my tits. I resent Mike, the prostitution, but most of all the strip club for operating a brothel and making me feel like a prude. In time, all the other San Francisco strip clubs follow suit by adopting and modifying management's illegal practices.

I remember a stripper telling me that giving hand-jobs wasn't sex.

I remember the rumor that management recruited the newly-arrived Asian immigrants from the massage parlors in the Tenderloin. But the Asian women aren't the only prostitutes up in the club. Nearly everyone is doing it. One day Baby, a petite slightly older Filipina, lets her customer blatantly stick his hand inside the front of her underwear. He does this out in the open area of the main audience—not even in the back rooms! I stare at Baby expecting she'll look up at some point but instead she ignores me. When I complain about it to Mike the manager, he replies, "Mind your own business." When I confront Baby in the dressing room, she throws a tantrum and screams, "How dare you! I would not do that! I have a husband! I'm married!" Someone forgot to send me the memo that married women don't prostitute. Tears stream down Baby's cheeks and she's poised to attack me but her Filipina friends restrain her and glare at me while cursing me out in Tagalog. Suddenly I am the asshole.

I remember Scarlet, the red-headed junkie with chiseled cheekbones whose skin glows unnaturally white who usually dances to metal. My favorite is when she wears fake glasses, hides her tattoos in a white button down shirt, tight short black skirt, and black opaque thigh highs to cover up her track marks. She strips to Van Halen's "Hot for Teacher" and during the climax, she rips the pencil out of her meticulously perfect bun and liberates her long red wavy tresses. After the $200 commission system went into effect, she'd show up for the last two hours of the night shift and miraculously make her money before vanishing off into the night like a vampire. I remember seeing Scarlet nod out one night on a customer's lap as he fingered her. I wonder if she's still alive.

I remember I'd show up drunk to work because there was no time to leisurely go to the bar on break anymore. It's incredibly stressful as I witness strippers turn tricks and fight feelings of hate with feeling sorry for them. I want to not care, but no amount of drugs or drinking sedate me enough to not feel the rage. One night I can't stomach it anymore. I'd wracked up a couple of hundred dollars in fees I "owed" the club from nights when I failed to make my $200 commission fee. It was illegal that they are charging us an inflated stage fee, let alone having us "owe" them money. I'm almost three hours into my shift and only have $120 from lap dancing. I find Mike the manager and flatly state, "I'm not going to give hand jobs to make my fee." He shakes his head and I could feel his coked out eyes glaze over me from behind his sunglasses as he laments, "You're not working with our system, Surina. This is going to be a problem." What system is that, Mike? The one where I become a prostitute in your stable for your pimp ass?

I don't remember what it felt like the first time a customer fondled my tits or the last. I cave in to this demand because it seems like a lesser evil to giving customers hand jobs, blow jobs or fucking them. I feel like a cow that is shocked so it passively goes to her slaughter with little or no resistance.

MY ALMOST FIRST TIME
Mandy Tz

This is the story of my (almost) first John, a name as fake as the one that I posted in the profile. "Hi Mandy," he wrote, "You're beautiful." He went on to describe himself at me, tossing progressively juicier bait so my sub-conscious would swim right where he wanted it to. "I am really into art and music. Darker stuff, hardcore stuff. I used to be very involved in the punk scene and I was no weekend warrior poser: I have the jail tattoos to prove it." Oh God, I thought, what if he's some sort of white supremacist? "But now I work as the VP for a non-profit that serves low income single mothers." Well that's a good sign ...hopefully. "I am into domination and ageplay: I want you to be my naughty little school girl who needs to be spanked. I am not gay—"

Hold it, brief break from the story. Guys, tricks, clients, whatever: you don't need to tell me you're straight. I get it. If you weren't straight you wouldn't be using a website that drops the words shemale and tranny like Obama drops the word hope. Anyways, back to the story.

"I just like girls like you. I was wondering if you'd like to meet up at a bar and we can talk about how this is going to work." A man who doesn't want a paper trail: I can respect that. But what if he tries to take me for a ride? I guess it's a bar, I can always scream for a bouncer.

I open the attachment on the email. It's a picture he took of himself by using the mirrored ceiling of an elevator. Oh, wannabe artsy types. But he was cute for a pasty white guy as old as my dad. So I thought, yeah sure why not. I told him I'd love to meet up. He said he could meet on Thursday night and I said I was free too. I didn't realize until Thursday morning that it was Valentine's Day. Hmmm, I wondered, should I be suspicious of that?

I hit up one of my girls who had been doing this sorta stuff for a while. "I wouldn't be worried," she told me in that tone of confident knowing that she spoke with even when she was clueless, "I've had lots of Valentine's bookings. They feel lonely. Hell, sometimes it means they will pay you more." Though I do ask for it, I am often wary of taking advice, especially on doing sex work, from cis girls. It is a completely different dynamic and though generally we are expected to be very similar things and to meet certain standards, trans women who detract in any way from those standards are judged much more harshly.

My outfit, makeup, legs, hair all have to be flawless, 'cause if and when my top comes off, my clients aren't happy to see the tiny little nibs. And this particular girl had, amongst other things, told me she had worked without makeup and had worked in flats, things I didn't and still don't think I could get away with. But for some reason I believed her this time. I was desperate to believe this would go smoothly: I had little money, my ex-girlfriend was kicking me out of our apartment, and I really wanted to get laid, even if the sex was shitty. I didn't want sex, I wanted affirmation that I would be okay.

One of the laundry list of reasons why my ex treated me like crap was my doing sex work. But my friends generally were very supportive, if worried and ignorant. I asked one of my friends if he could be my emergency contact for this session and he said yes. I later found out that he promptly got drunk, fucked his girlfriend, and passed out.

So when I texted him when I got to the bar he never responded, and this was the first thing that made me nervous. I was late and worse had run into friends at the train stop who gave me unspoken judgment for going out alone on Valentine's dressed like a Mötley Crüe groupie. But John was there: good, I hate waiting for anything ever. He said hi, asked me what I wanted to drink. I said I'd have whatever he's having. He showed me an AA token. Bad sign number two. I told him whiskey on the rocks. He was impressed. I was unimpressed by him being impressed: girls drink whiskey, boys; get over it. We went to a quiet back room of the bar. He told me he'd like to have a couple of drinks and talk, then take a cab back to his place. Once we were in the cab he'd give me my fee, which I was pleased to hear was higher than what I was going to ask for. I turned on my teen girl ditzy "Oh my god you're so interesting; please tell me more forever" act. But this time it was hard; maybe it was 'cause it was the first time I had done this sort of thing with a client (it was a bit more intimate than webcamming or phone sex) or maybe it was cause he was actually incredibly likable. When he talked about his life, it actually sounded like someone I wouldn't mind going out with.

But he kept asking about me. Too much about me. Asking where I lived (lied), what my family is like (lied), what work I did besides this (lie, lie, lie). It was making me really uncomfortable, lying this much. I am a great liar, specifically when I have little to no respect for the people I am lying to; I view it as that they do not deserve to hear the truth from me. But it was hard to think that about John; I wanted to complain to him about my ex, wanted to tell him how lonely I was, wanted to tell him how I felt like a liar every time my mom asked me if I was okay financially.

So I pulled my wild card too soon: in the middle of him going off about how his girlfriend left him after she caught him looking at tranny porn (at least 30% of clients will tell me some variation of this story) I jumped on top of his lap and started making out with him. And thank Baphomet that I am so shallow and have such high standards in sexual partners, because as soon as he started that fucking propeller tongue shit that straight dudes just love to do I thought, "Yep you're just a client."

It was starting to get pretty heated, large wandering hands quickly figuring out the small expanse of my body. Bringing me in, but the affirmation wasn't there. I still knew that I had been kicked out. It wasn't working. Well, nothing is more affirming than drinking by yourself on Valentine's. So I stopped, leaned back, and said in a sultry voice dripping with lust, "Hey let's get out of here." But he didn't want to go just yet, he wanted to talk more. I looked at him with the sweetest look I could muster (whilst the voices in my head yelled, "Bitch I got a fucking handle of Captain at home I don't want to spend all night listening to the tragedy that is your fucked up fetish.") and said, "Sugar, we both know why I'm here. I do really like you, but this is work. I'm a pro. It's time to do this or start paying for the conversation too."

I am not good at a lot of things. Cooking? Nope. Gardening? Kill everything I touch. Mechanical stuff? No thanks. Making people cry? Oh I wish it were an Olympic event. Whether it is my parents, my teachers, my friends, my partners, complete strangers, bosses, co-workers, and most of all straight white people, my straightforward no-bullshit if you don't like it you can suck my girly dick attitude turns on the waterworks for people. And here it came: he is so lonely, it is Valentine's Day, he was hoping after we had talked for so long that it might mean something more. I just kept that sweet understanding expression on my face cause I knew if I budged it an inch my "What the fuck?" face would takeover forever. I just kept repeating sorry and that we needed to go or he needed to pay up now. So he got out his wallet. "I only have $60, is that enough?"

I did this, I thought in the brief few seconds before my emotions took over, I burned myself. "What?" I almost yelled. "What the fuck do you mean $60? What about the money you were going to pay me after the cab ride?"

"Well I was hoping that-"

"Excuse me? Do you understand what my life is? Mister fucking VP? This shit ain't free. This shit ain't ever free." I snatched the $60 out of his hand.

"Let me call you a cab home..."

"Fuck you asshole, get lost."

I cried all the way home. It was the loneliest train ride though there were a few people apprehensively glaring at the sobbing wreck before them. No one to tell me about the old punk shows at C Squat. No one to tell me they forgive me, I don't have to be kicked out.

New York City is the busiest, most crowded place I've ever been. And it really bums me out on nights like this one. I called and texted, messaged and looked: it was Valentine's Day so all my friends were out having a good time with their partners or had already passed out in a state of inebriation and self-pity. This story doesn't have a happy ending, and for most girls like me they normally don't. We don't get the chance to be sex worker positive: because I can't tell stories like this one and have them end on some "And that's how I stuck up for myself and defeated the patriarchy!" bullshit, I get labeled as a tragic travesty. John emailed me the next day apologizing, saying that he knows I was right and that he was going to abstain from prostitutes forever. I really do think he meant it in a nice way, but it was salt in the wounds. It was a "Look at you, you cold bitch: you just pushed away your meal ticket." Just as I had pushed away my ex, my friends, my family. Fearing my feelings, choosing sex work because I thought it would be a job where my cold, calculating attitude would be appreciated.

I got my fourth rejection from a porno company that day, telling me to come back in a year once my tits were bigger. Ironically this place said it wanted models with all body types. But what they meant was they wanted cis models with all body types. They want to buy the sex of cis girls, they want me to be their free Valentine's treat and shoulder to cry on. I wanted chocolates and instead I was given dead roses. I go out to buy my own and they are sold out. I try to make my own and I burn myself. I burn myself. I burn myself.

GEMINI'S TWINS
Dominick

I turned forty in 2004, which was a super busy year for me, working freelance meeting planning gigs—mostly dinners at upscale restaurants for doctors being wooed by pharmaceutical companies—and turning tricks. I'd gotten into escorting the year before, after a very persistent guy on the Upper West Side offered me money to meet up with him. At first I thought I was too old, but after getting some glowing online reviews, I was booked every week. My career as an escort was just hitting its stride, and I was determined to meet my monthly sales goals. I held on to the freelance events gig because it was a good cover story, and it kept one foot in the door of a so-called "legit" field. Although in retrospect, I'm pretty sure providing men with intimate touch by the hour is way more legit that pimping drugs over steak dinners.

One spring day, in the midst of this very busy period, I awoke with the awareness that I couldn't see out of one half of one eye, the right eye, the bottom half. Having crashed out in my contact lenses a couple of times that week (I'd normally remove them each night) I thought maybe this was due to a lens having gotten folded up and stuck behind my eye. I pulled on my lid and rolled my eyeball around a couple of times while looking down, expecting a lost disc of plastic to fall out and restore my sight. When that didn't work, I put off dealing with the problem and just burned through my day.

I ignored the situation for a couple of more days. I was morbidly fascinated with the darkness. If I forced myself I could look through it. I thought the curved horizon line between sight and blackness was beautiful. The blackness wasn't all that black, more like oxblood. One afternoon, my errands took me past an eye clinic in Chelsea, and I thought I'd stop in to see if they could get that stray contact lens out. I explained what was going on, and was quickly shuttled from the receptionist to the intake nurse to the head ophthalmologist, a Greek with soap opera star good looks. At a certain moment, their attention on me turned very serious.

"You have a torn retina, and need emergency surgery—immediately," the handsome Greek ophthalmologist explained.

Luckily, the tear was on the lower half of the retina, meaning that loose portion of my retina was gently flapping around in vitreous fluid, the gel that normally fills the space between lens and retina. Had the tear been on the upper half, gravity would likely have taken its course, and the retina would have peeled off, leaving me blind in that eye.

There is a beautiful mosaic tile wall at the entrance to the New York Eye and Ear Infirmary on Second Avenue, vivid blue and green hues in the mid-century style. My assigned eye surgeon, Uri Shabto, was a redheaded Jew of compact, muscled physique. He sensed my panic over my predicament, and lied to me sweetly, telling me the procedure was completely routine, and I'd be fully recovered in a couple of weeks. This soothed my nerves, because I was worried that being out of commission for too long would slow my momentum. I was also looking forward to throwing a party for my fortieth birthday, a month away. I sensed he was downplaying because I was so freaked out, but accepted his soothing tale. He was one of the innovators of the procedure, I was told. My mom and dad rushed into the city to be with me, and I was knocked out with a heavy sedative.

I came to in the recovery room with both eyes bandaged, I guess because it's hard to bandage just one eye. The nurses were all Filipina, and I was flying so high that I believed I could speak and understand Tagalog, but those nurses were having none of it. After failing to convince them that I could speak their native language, I blurted out: "Nurse? NURSE! You don't understand. I've been in recovery for six years and this sedative is making me REALLY! HIGH! RIGHT! NOW!" My mom and dad were standing at my bedside in the recovery room and that's how I told them I was in a recovery program— while tripping out on propofol.

Once I came back to my senses, I had a nice chat with them about my addiction and my recovery, about which they knew absolutely nothing. I was always good at hiding. They took me home to Long Island and my mom attended to me. I lay in bed super uncomfortable and bored, unable to write, watch TV, turn over, or even masturbate—just prolonged, sightless introspection. Every day for weeks following the procedure, my mom lifted the bandages to administer one drop once in the morning, another three times a day, and yet another five times a day. One was for pain, one was a steroid and the other was an antibiotic, I think. My dad came in one day to tell me that he'd asked Doctor Shabto pointed questions about the procedure, and the Doctor, who had lied to me so fluently, told my dad that for the procedure, my eyeball had been removed from the socket and set to rest on my cheek. That was probably why my right eye looked twice the size of my left and like it was filled with raspberry jam for weeks after.

I returned to my East Village apartment after almost a month of convalescence. The surgery was a success in that it saved my eyesight, and for that I was very grateful. But the whole incident really put a dent in my birthday plans. I was flat broke from being out of work, and soft from lying in bed all month; my prospects seemed lamentable. When I let some of my regulars know what had happened, and that I was still wearing an eye patch, they said it sounded sexy, but I just felt broken, flabby, and vulnerable.

I'd been off the radar for the last month, and the prospect of throwing a birthday party for myself with just a few days to put it together (and no money) looked dim, too. Many of my friends were already at the beach for the season, a place that was strictly off limits to me. One grain of sand could ruin everything. I was settling into my sad pirate despair when I got a call from Felix. Felix was a really cute guy from San Francisco. He'd come to town for the US Open the year prior, and I met him in his room at the Hudson Hotel and gave him a wild, swinging night. He called me with an odd request. He explained that his sister ran a fashion courier business out of JFK Airport, and they needed a courier for a last-minute job. Did I know anybody who was available to fly to Barcelona tomorrow, to deliver a dress and a pair of shoes? They'd be put up in a hotel for a couple of days, and receive a small stipend.

Nothing was keeping me in New York; if I took the courier gig, I'd spend my birthday in Barcelona. I checked to make sure my passport was handy. I called my eye surgeon and asked if I could fly and he said yes, just don't go to the beach. I called Felix's sister and negotiated a five-day stay and enough cash to book a hostel and cover my expenses.

The next afternoon a car service picked me up and drove me to the courier's offices, adjacent to the airport. I met Felix's sister and she gave me a garment bag and a shoebox to take with my carry-on luggage. This is how fashion couriers work; it's faster and more reliable to pay someone to take the merchandise on the plane as their own luggage, rather than send it as commercial goods, and have to deal with customs. She handed me my tickets and about five hundred dollars. "You will be delivering this to Fabrizio Moretti at the Hotel Arts in Barcelona" she said.

That name rang a bell. Isn't he the drummer for the Strokes? His name had been in the news lately for some reason. I fly to Barcelona that night and after a change of planes at Charles de Gaulle, arrive the next afternoon, sweaty, dirty, and one-eyed. I jump in a taxi to my destination, a tall, newish luxury hotel on the Mediterranean, adjacent to the Olympic Village.

I hustle into the lobby with the garment bag and shoebox—my "must deliver by" time is fast approaching—and ask for Mr. Moretti at the reception desk. I hear a familiar woman's voice behind me say "Oh yay! You made it." I turn around and it's Drew Barrymore, in a pretty yellow dress. She's petite, and radiantly beautiful; everyone in her proximity is smiling and a little awestruck. She takes the garment bag from me and gives me an affectionate hug. She smells like fresh cut flowers, and I can only guess what I smell like. We make some small talk—the dress I'd brought over is for her to wear to a friend's wedding—and I'm on my way, job completed.

I have an amazing time cautiously exploring Barcelona for the next five days, eye patch and all. At one point as I'm walking along the seafront in Barceloneta, a young boy points at me and says "Mira Papi, un pirata!" and his father calmly responds "Si, es un pirata." On the eve of my birthday, I go to a nightclub, dance all night with cute Catalan boys, and then go home with one, a skinny kid with a Mohawk, named Ferran. We have a hushed romp in his room- he has two roommates, one on either side of him, and they both have to get up early for work. I awake to the three of them having breakfast at the small kitchen table. Ferran's roommates are identical twins. One works for the phone company and the other works for the sanitation department, and they are both dressed in their respective uniforms. It's the morning of my fortieth birthday, I'm a Gemini, and I'm having coffee with impossibly sexy blue-collar Catalan identical twin brothers.

The twins say their goodbyes – they are very friendly, and affectionate with Ferran. I look to Ferran to shed some light on this situation, and he shrugs. They are his roommates, nothing more, they are super nice guys, they know he is gay, they are totally cool with it, no they are not gay, yes they are impossibly sexy, and no, he does not know how he sleeps every night in the room between theirs.

So despite the emergency eye surgery and the heavy dose of sedative and the inopportune revelation of my past addiction and my loss of nearly a month to convalescence and the corresponding loss of income, I had a sublime fortieth birthday, taking a completely unexpected, all-expenses-paid trip to an enchanted Mediterranean city, thanks to Doctor Shabto, Felix from San Francisco, the fashion industry, jet travel, Pollux, Castor, all the stars on the eastern horizon, Drew Barrymore, Ferran, his hot roommates, and God.

LAP DANCE CLASS
Essence Revealed

I couldn't fall asleep. The visions of protesters standing outside my lap dance workshop at the University of Colorado as part of the week long residency with Gesel Mason's show, "Women, Sex & Desire: Sometimes You Feel Like a Ho Sometimes You Don't" were so vivid. I feared what my imagination would transform the visions into during my slumber. Without a doubt, nightmare would be my imagination's dream-making genre of choice. Grotesque exaggerations of characters like the protesters outside of Planned Parenthood danced in my head. Why did I agree to teach a lap dance workshop to university level dance majors? I already had a fear of teaching "real dancers." Plus, Gesel told us that there was already one student (who had experience as a club stripper) who had called in her concern and disapproval to the dance department about it. She told the department, "There is NOTHING empowering about giving a lap dance." And she said she had firsthand experience of doing them for work. The metaphysical side of my intellect failed in its attempts to coach my mind. Intellect was hearing none of metaphysical's warnings that this type of vivid visualization would only manifest it into reality.

I can see my detractor setting up the final details of the protest that both I and the participants of my class will have to walk through. There are almost thirty students signed up. I think it's safe to estimate that only half will actually show up. Perhaps even half of that half, if the protesters assemble and shame them away. I fight sleep as long as I can.

Why didn't I campaign harder to teach a theater workshop instead? I was hired as a part of this modern dance/conversation piece to be the wordsmith. As the only actor (and not classically trained dancer), I deliver the monologues. I barely dance. Choreography and the specificity trained dancers move with terrify me. I'm a classically trained actor with an MA in Educational Theater not in fighting protesters averse to sensual dance styles.

When I wake up in the morning, I cannot remember my dream. Did I even have one? It's a way too early morning hour for my night owl self. As part of the residency at the university, we taught classes all week. Despite my difficult night, I get up and go into the 8 am choreography class, then many of the other dance workshops being taught by the dancers in the show. There are no protests happening at any of their classes. I'm jealous.

Evening arrives. The entire cast goes into the large studio where my workshop will take place. I don't have to walk through a line of angry protesters. I focus on setting up my MP3s which are filled with old music I like to groove to. Three students trickle in. I'm relieved that anyone has shown up. A few more students trickle in. Thankfully, one of my professional dancer cast mates agrees to lead the warm up. I've led the cast through the class to practice, so she knows which muscles need to be revved up and stretched out. I focus on my own breathing. By the time the warm up ends, there are almost thirty women in the circle. The most I've ever done this workshop with up to this point is fifteen women.

One of the first things I have them do post warm up is close their eyes and run their fingertips down the front of their bodies starting at the forehead. My cast members told me they were shocked in my audition when I actually touched my breasts because in dance training they are told NOT to touch themselves sexually. So, I watched to see what they would do. I watched them graze armpits when they got to their breasts.

I reminded them that their armpits are not on the front of their bodies and that this is not classical dance. "Touch your breasts, they're yours! Keep your eyes closed and the focus on yourself." They laugh. Most manage to do it. We go through dance moves to be done on the floor, standing, with a chair and then intro to booty twerk. I've learned that trained dancers get the twerk moves quicker than most newcomers. I wonder if it's because they study the body and anatomy. I had warned them that it may not happen right away. By the end of the class, I am hoarse. We are all a giddy giggle fest of ladies cheering for each other through improvised solos. The protesters never showed.

The next night our teaching residency was over. The week culminated in the students we'd worked with in classrooms the past seven days and university community at large seeing our show. The student who called in her concern about my class would be in attendance. Before the show begins, the creator of the piece leads us in exercises. This show is part modern dance, part interactive conversation. Random strangers from the audience are paired up. Cast members always participate as well. We always pair up with people from the audience as opposed to working with each other. My partner this time is a tall woman wearing cool wedged heel boots with a fountain of blonde waves spilling from her head.

I'm always impressed by the audience members who are willing to do these exercises sight unseen. They are never done without consent but are physical and can involve a stranger's touch. We face each other making eye contact for a few breaths. I ask, "Do I have permission to put your hand on one of my vulnerable spots?" She nods yes. I place her hand on my right hip. We maintain eye contact for a few breaths. She then places my hand on the right side of her neck. We maintain eye contact for a few breaths. I place her hand on the left side of my lower back. She places my hand on her belly. As we continue we then use body to body contact. My head on her shoulder for a few breaths. Her knee is on mine. At one point we are hip to hip and back to back.

My intention is always to remain open and empathetic. Being an art school graduate, I've spent years being physically and emotionally open with virtual strangers. Eye contact is a rarity in city life. As a New Yorker, this is something that is very seldom encountered, especially with a stranger. When we are signaled to wrap up, I thank my partner. We hug and she returns to her seat. Then the show begins. We are seated in the round for many rows. Gesel starts the conversation by asking for initial thoughts upon hearing the show title.

People speak out their responses: "I'm not a ho."

"Yeah, that's about right."

"The Almond Joy song..."

Each conversation leads into a choreographed dance number or monologue. I am open and present with the cast and the audience. When dancing at a strip club, I can be making a grocery list or thinking about how many to-do list items were accomplished that day. Here nothing is rote. Each audience and conversation is different. I laugh; I cry; I feel; I love it.

At the end of the show, I'm shocked to find out that my partner was the concerned student, unbeknownst to both of us. I asked Gesel to point the potential protester out to me after the show.

Gesel described what she looks like, "Tall, blonde wavy hair."

"With the cool wedge boots," I ask?

"Yes."

"She was my partner during the warm up!!!" The woman I spent the better part of the week terrified of ended up being one I hugged in gratitude for taking part in the "vulnerable spots" exercise.

After the show, she waited as other audience members came up to me to talk. We made eye contact and there was an unspoken agreement that we would talk before leaving the space. I walked over to her when I was finally able to.

She said, "Thank you for sharing your story. I'm a feminist. I feel like I did things and went places I really didn't want to so I could make money. I hated every minute of stripping when I did it. It never dawned on me that anyone could like it. But hearing your story, I can see how everyone's experiences can be different."

"Yeah, I had my good nights and bad but I feel like it was a good option for me. I learned pretty fast that it wasn't worth it to do something I was uncomfortable with…"

"And I hated talking to them: 'What's your real name? What are you doing here? I'd rather spend money taking you to dinner. Blah, blah, blah.'" She repeats, "I hated talking to them."

We both laugh, and I sympathize with her. "I know right? I felt like a broken record sometimes giving the same answers every night all night. But, in general, I like talking to customers. My favorite ones are the ones who like to pay me to just sit and talk."

"Ugh, no thanks! I'd rather just dance and not have to say anything to them."

She had hated customers looking at her and dealing with the rejection all night. I reveled in the freedom to be nearly naked in public. The rejection was never fun but as an actor, "no," was something that I had had to make peace with. No two experiences even within the same realm are ever exactly the same.

It is these types of moments that make the choice to live life as an artist of incalculable value. I'm grateful to her for our in-common exchanges of being human despite the vast differences in experiences we had of being sex workers. Viva la différence, and our commonalities, both.

LANGUAGE OF SURVIVAL
Lily Fury

"There's close enough and too far," she says. "You always want to go too far."

Silence breeds unwanted agreement. I gave up my cells for this, 'cause I wanted to know. 'Cause I wanted to feel what it was like to bleed the way you bled. She ran to carry me with her arms outstretched, in her army uniform with patches bearing her name that they stole from her. I buried my heart, heavy as bricks, as she held me like a small child and ran her fingers through my hair.

All strung out on her beauty and love, I had to say goodbye to her. But her philosophical words couldn't save us from our present time/space realities.

She will get blood on her uniform from reviving soldiers in the war. They will fly all of her beauty away.

She spoke to me in whispers of our futures intertwined. When she is free she will take me to her homeland and teach me to dance the South Caribbean way.

But now I am hidden to her like a past secret from a past life that she doesn't want to remember, she pushed my lips away from hers. We are surrounded by uniforms.

Flashback to the first day I met her; I was negotiating my terms with a large woman with demons in her eyes. Later, I found out that the girls called her snake lady.

"I don't want to fuck," I told her.

"Fine, then you can do massage for now, but by next week you'll be on your back like all the rest of the girls, it's where the real money is at. Don't nobody think you special." She scribbled down an address for me and gave me cab fare, she told me there was only one other girl on shift that night and that she would let me inside. When I got there, the door was open. It was a decrepit little third-floor walkup apartment in the Bronx. There were three bedrooms with just a single mattress in each and nothing else. I could hear a trick moaning in the other room: "Mmm baby, that feels so good, yeah bitch I like it like that." All I hear from her is silence. The walls are thin and flaking away. The florescent light is flickering. He moans wildly like he's about to explode. I turn up my Walkman louder; I might be a mess but I sure can survive.

When she's done she showed him out and then came into my room and sat on my mattress with me. She was beautiful. Deep dark eyes so easy to get lost in, full lips, caramel skin and thick dark hair that ran down her back.

"I think he was to have a heart attack, " she said in her very broken English.

I was laughing until I looked up and saw that she was scared, and serious.

"What's your name?" I asked her.

"Dia Jar," she said.

She looked at me real closely, examining and memorizing my face, she shyly asked if she could touch my hair.

"Sure," I said.

She apologized, laughing. She said that it was just that she had never seen a white person up close before.

I laughed, "Never?" I asked.

"Only on the TV," she answered.

She told me her story. She was from the Dominican Republic; it was her first day working. Her baby son was back in her country and he was sick. She needed to get the best possible treatment for her son and couldn't afford it on what she was making there. She was a philosophy teacher in her country, she wanted a better life for both of her sons and to get away from her abusive husband.

After a slew of clients had passed through and the night was winding down, Dia Jar and I sat together talking. In the midst of our conversation we heard an abrupt rapping at the front door. Snake lady hadn't called to inform me of any appointments, which was the procedure. Dia Jar and I looked at each other, surprised. It was getting dark outside. I tiptoed to the front door in my lingerie and peeked through the window. All I see are flashlights, guns, and blue uniforms. Fuck.

"We have to go," I told Dia Jar, flustered and anxious.

"Policia?" she asked.

"Si," I responded quickly.

She started to cry. She was in danger of being deported as she wasn't a resident and was only here on some sort of vacation visa. I wiped the tears from her eyes. We could cry later. We had to get out immediately. I opened the window, snatched the money I had made that night and a small bag. We were both still in our lingerie. It was a long way down. Farther than I had expected. Dia Jar gasped as she looked down.

"Don't look down," I told her. She was starting to tremble. "Close your eyes," I told her. She did.

She held my hands as we jumped together. Maybe there were angels looking out for us that night because all that remained from that jump were cuts and bruises.

"Are you okay?" I asked her as we slowly got up and collected ourselves. She nodded. We were halfway down the street when Dia Jar realized she had left her money from that night in her room in the midst of all the chaos. She was still holding my hand. I quickly took my stack of money out and handed her half.

"No," she said.

"Yes!" I insisted. "Walk up that way," I told her, pointing, "you'll be able to hail a cab." I kissed her forehead and started to run.

"Lily!" she called out. I turned back for a split second.

"Thank you!" she yelled, and from that day, me and Dia Jar were inseparable. Sharing secrets, learning about each other's pasts and our hopes for the future. I remember ransacking every bookstore in Manhattan to find her favorite philosophers in Spanish and the happiness that radiated from her as she embraced me when I gave them to her. One fateful day she had called me and told me she wanted to meet up because she had something to talk to me about. Her voice was shaking.

"Tell me now," I insisted, upset.

"I'm going to join the army," she told me.

I started to cry and could hear her crying as well.

"They will make me a citizen and help me bring my children here," she said.

"They don't give a fuck about you," I told her, frustrated.

"Lily please don't be upset. I love you," she cried. She didn't have the luxury of choice, she had babies running wild and sick back in her country and a brutal husband she wanted to escape.

"You could die," I told her.

"Ms. Lily," she said, lowering her voice as she said calmly, "It's better to die once and stay dead than to die every day and then have to get back up and fuck again."

Silence at the end of my line. All the fight I had left in me died at that moment and I just sank into the cold tiles of the bathroom floor and cried. The whoring was killing her and now the army will own her but these CEOs and these Wall Street fucks that steal a piece of her every time. They don't know her soul like I do, or that she has enough love in her heart to stop every war.

And now, I was here visiting her on her army training base in Texas, but the visit was up. She had tears in her eyes saying goodbye, but through all her struggle, she still never lost her smiles or her glow. A survivalist. I stepped outside with all of the loneliness in the world weighing on my heart.

I had to leave her. She walked me to the car and drew something with her finger in the dust. Before I left, I looked to see what she had drawn. It was a yin-yang. I beamed. My philosophy teacher, reminding me of the perfect balance of good and bad in existence. I kissed her cheek and rode away into the night.

PTSD
Dion P. Scott

I was bored with working in TV and film production, doing extra work and auditioning all day to become an actor, waiting for my big break. The unbearable suffering I was living with from post-traumatic stress disorder had left me with depression, paranoia, anxiety, and insomnia. It was too much to bear. I endured a physical attack in 1997 after giving some trade a ride home. Being a naive good Samaritan left me drugged with a broken jaw, handcuffed, and riddled with three gunshot wounds. The attack and attempted rape desensitized me to violence. I was already forced to deal with the fear of death so what could be worse? Often times suicidal, I didn't know how to cope. I became like a zombie and just needed an escape. I enjoyed sex, so I figured that would be the best medicine for me. I started to crave some excitement and danger in my life. I wanted to experience the seedier, grimy dark side. I had found that pursuing a professional Hollywood career was extremely boring. I didn't enjoy acting and the entertainment industry as much as I thought I would. The pretentiousness was too much for me. I wanted to write my own script and create a fun, scary, adventurous life for myself to escape the mental anguish I was in constantly.

So, I took what I had learned from my acting classes and experience in TV and film production and became a late night street walker cruising for dick. I created Miss Tasha, my alter ego who got to do and say stuff that the boy version of me didn't have the balls to.

Tasha got away with certain things because she used her femininity to her full advantage, and through Tasha I discovered how femininity could disarm men and be used to manipulate them. I hit the streets as Tasha only after sundown, as I was too ashamed and embarrassed to venture out in daylight looking like a girl.

I had zero confidence in the beginning. Besides, men were much more horny and willing to play after sundown and the freaks have always been known to come out at night. As sunset approached, I would wait anxiously, eager to play dress up and to let Tasha out of the house. I seduced men into sex for the pure fun of it, honed my skills and perfected my craft, enjoyed my newfound freedom as a bitch. First, I started out in my local neighborhood, near La Brea and Olympic in early 2000. I learned how to apply makeup: eyeliner was my all time favorite, along with lipgloss to accentuate my lips while sucking on blow pops. I would wear a pair of pants with a long, untucked shirt. I cut the butt cheeks out of my pants, kind of like the notorious outfit Prince wore on stage in the 80s. I loved the reaction I got from men when I would pull my shirt up and expose my butt cheeks: it drove some men crazy and they loved it, others hated it and would chase and threaten me.

My favorite spot to stand was at a bus stop, late at night in front of a gas station. I would act like I was waiting for a bus. Guys would cruise by, offer me rides, and feel sorry for me.

"You want a ride baby?" was usually their pickup line.

"No, my bus should be here soon, thank you!" Or I would just walk away, or flat out ignore them if I wasn't interested. If the guy was cute, I would jump in and say "How can I repay you for being so kind'? They would usually start giggling. And when I saw cute guys pumping their gas, I would try and seduce them, though it didn't always work. But I often hit the jackpot and felt very accomplished when a guy was receptive to my advances.

Weekends were the best because all the men would be on their way back home from the Hollywood area, coming out of the clubs horny and drunk. La Brea Avenue was a long stretch and went from Hollywood all the way down to Inglewood, not far from the Los Angeles Airport. I lived in the Mid-Wilshire area, a business and residential area full of working class folks, a large number of them entertainment professionals. The Screen Actors Guild, our union, was literally around the corner from my home.

I had to get used to boys flirting with me and coming on to me when I was dressed as a girl. About 70 percent of the time, I told them I was not a real female. Some didn't understand, so I had to tell them I didn't have a vagina. I was amazed they didn't understand. I didn't even have breasts but my face was feminine enough and the girl clothes and the wig gave a good enough illusion to seduce them. Boys didn't care, they just wanted a hole to stick it in, its not like we were getting married. Once I realized that I would have more opportunities to have sex with boys if I dressed up as a girl, this became my number one pastime. I suddenly had men propositioning me constantly, offering me money and drugs whenever I was out dressed as a girl. I realized it came with the territory: if you're on the trans feminine spectrum it's just assumed that you're a ho. Guys would always ask me, "How much?" I remember one time this guy asked me and I was not in the mood and I spit in his face. It used to make me mad because at the beginning I just wanted to have casual sex, but it was like they forced you into being a ho. When I realized men wanted to pay me, I started gladly taking their money and became much more professional. I guess I accidentally became a ho.

After about 3 years of playing in my local neighborhood, it was time to move on because I had become too popular from my late night antics of flashing my ass. Things were getting out of control; boys would start popping up at my apartment wanting sex again, leaving notes on my door, waiting outside for me to leave my home.

Several attacked me late at night and forced me to give them what they wanted. Others threatened me, saying that if I didn't have sex with them they would tell the police I was the midnight flasher, the one who was always at the gas station flashing my ass. It was only a matter of time before I would have been hurt much worse. I decided to venture up to Hollywood where other transvestites, transsexuals, and transgender women worked.

My life changed once I set foot on the ho stroll. I decided to work as a girl because I already knew there was money to be made. I just got way better results, so there was no need to stop pretending to be a girl; working as a boy would have been boring and futile to me. Besides, as a boy, gay men didn't want me because I was too feminine and pretty. I was never boyish or masculine enough for them.

The men who were attracted to me when I was Tasha identified as heterosexual, though really, I didn't care how they identified, as long as they had a hard dick for me and didn't hurt me. Their identity was their business, not mine. Working the stroll was both financially rewarding and extremely sexually satisfying. I knew I belonged on the streets once I got broken in. Santa Monica Boulevard was my refuge; it was total freedom; it was like a big playground.

My apartment in Hollywood was about a 20 minute walk to Santa Monica Boulevard. I slept most of the day and went to the YMCA to relax and chill. I took care of various routine normal day-to-day business appointments, as I did not want to completely drop out of society.

At sundown, my ass was headed to work. The boulevard was like a freeway, cars constantly speeding up and down the large, four-lane street. It was an area that became very festive at night and had a carnival atmosphere, with a club in the area called Circus, and Latino men hustling their hot dog carts. This was the same exact area years earlier where I had started my TV and film production career. I now knew what it was like to be one of them, standing on the corners, waiting for a customer to turn a trick.

The cops would ride around, harassing us. Some were even bold enough to call us over to their squad cars and be stroking their dicks. I guess with all the sexual energy and opportunities out there, no man could resist the temptation of hos spread out on corner after corner, all the misfits hoping to make enough cash to get through the night, or meet a man who would take care of them. It was said that usually after two or three years, the precinct would rotate the cops out of the vice squad because they became corrupt, engaging in the very practices they were meant to police. Tuesdays and Thursdays were known to be vice night, everyone would be more careful than usual.

The corner I worked near a gas station was my favorite corner, off of Santa Monica Boulevard and Vine Street. I felt safe there and I preferred to work by myself. I did not care to have other girls around me for too long. I positioned myself on the corner so I could see all the main traffic on the boulevard and any cars that were coming down the side street. Safety was always my number one concern. It came easy for me to turn tricks since I had no issues with standing on street corners or dealing with strangers.

I already had years of experience with this because at a young age I had been forced to do so--but instead of selling my ass as a kid, I was hustling Jehovah's Witness literature. As a young child I had been conditioned to stand on corners announcing god's kingdom, interacting with and engaging the public. This must have prepared me for the real street work. Now I was just doing something much more intimate, at night, and with an extremely different wardrobe! As a Jehovah's Witness there was a script to go by and you had to be prepared to interact with the public. Hustling on the corner at night was similar, just a different product and script.

Guys drove up, I looked at them, they looked at me, they pulled over, I approached the car and said, "Hi, what's up?" in my best girly voice. I would say, "Hey daddy, what you got for me? If you want me to be a good girl you gone have to treat me right, daddy, I got the best ass pussy out here."

And they usually kept it to the point, and asked, "How much?" If we agreed, they would say, "Get in." It generally took no longer than one minute to agree to the terms of what would be done to make them happy. Sold, deal done, next.

A certain amount of trust was involved: I had to hope the date was respectful and not a cop, but he was also hoping that I was not a cop and that I was respectful. There were plenty of men to go around to feed my appetite for sex and attention, and they were paying money--this was all so unbelievable. I got hooked, and this nighttime adventure turned into a full time career, an unexplainable profession. With all the money coming in and the attention, there was no turning back to my regular life; that was history. I started to go out street hustling, night after night, trick after trick.

I carried plenty of condoms and lubrication, they were essential for the job's functions. Hanging out until just before sun up, pounding the pavement, waiting to serve the straight men, anxiously hoping the guy would be cute with a big dick and some good ass for me, sometimes I didn't even care about the money! The number of handsome men paying for sex always made my jaws drop in more ways than one. Half of the time I was having sex for free. Had the other hos known that, they would have killed me.

I was constantly trolling the boulevard in search of that next piece of dick, the way a crack head trolls for crack in the wee hours of the morning. My behavior was so erratic, guys often would ask me what was I on and I would reply, "Nothing," and I was being honest! I wanted to live a normal life, but with my past experiences, normalcy was nowhere around me.

This went on for about four years, but then there was a turning point. I was deep throating a date, but the date wanted to fuck me in the car, and I told him I was not ready. He got mad, but didn't say anything, as I was choking on his dick, doing my job, the nigga reached across me, pulled a gun out of the passenger side door, held it to my forehead and said, "You faggot ass nigga, give me my fucking money back and empty your pockets!"

I quickly obliged, gave him his 40 bucks back, and told him, "Daddy, I'm not gone fight, just be nice to me ok?" I knew it was important to be submissive, but was ready to take control if need be. I exited the car with no gunshots fired. The nigga drove off as I cursed him out: "You faggot ass punk, I'm a get you nigga, I'm get you nigga. Don't let me see you back out here; I got your license plates!" I was so mad and ready to set it off. But I went right back to work; there were too many men who wanted my attention to focus on that nigga.

During the last year I worked Santa Monica Boulevard, I started taking female hormones, estrogen shots administered by my doctor. I had health insurance, so I didn't have to use money from turning tricks to pay for them the way other girls did. I also started getting silicone shots in my buttocks to fatten up my booty and to give it a more plump, feminine look.

It took years to work up the courage to get silicone injections as knew the risk, but I knew the power of having a big booty as well. I got laser hair removal treatments over several years so I wouldn't have to deal with nasty razor bumps. But the more I became feminine, taking female hormones, it reaffirmed to me that I didn't want to live full time as a woman. Making more money and starting to work out of my home was a new adventure as well.

I knew I was not transgender; I identified as a boy, as a gay male. I just knew if I feminized myself even more that my chances at making more money and meeting more hot guys would multiply. I became addicted to the attention and adulation I got from guys, but soon realized it's true; they say: anything to get some ass!

I started attempting to get back into mainstream, respectable work, weaning myself from the streets, while living in West Hollywood with my English bulldog, Kina.

I met a gentleman. When he picked me up, he said his name was Andre. He was a tall, muscular, jock type. He had big hands, big feet, and was dark chocolate with a full mustache and goatee. On the back of his truck he had a Los Angeles Fire Department sticker.

He was my knight in shining armor. I remember the first time we met, the sun was coming up and the birds had just started chirping. Something was telling me to stay out a little longer as I was not ready to go home. It was extremely unusual for me to stay in the streets past sun up; nighttime was ok but during the daytime turning tricks, *hell NO!*

A Ford Expedition with tinted windows cruised me a couple of times. I was very happy when I saw the driver and immediately knew I would like him. He liked my ass and that's what he wanted. He had seen me flashing the guys my booty. He gave me 40 bucks and said he liked it African style. I knew what that meant. We went into some bushes, and after two or three minutes, he nutted—quick and done.

About two weeks went by and I was back at my same routine. It was a routine that I could perform in my sleep: I would bend over, acting like I dropped something and my butt cheeks would just be hanging out. Guys would be honking their horns, some folks would ride by and throw stuff at me, was constantly dodging eggs and bottles. So I'm at it and Andre the firefighter picks me up again. "This time," I say, "let's go to my house so we could be more comfortable."

Andre was very, very cheap; he never gave me more than 40 bucks, even though I made him feel like a million. But still, I knew he really liked me because when he kissed me it was so passionate,; he would just hold me in his arms and gaze into my eyes. He was about six feet two, and I enjoyed looking up at him, being held in his arms. He started dropping by in the early mornings and bringing me my favorite breakfast from Jack in the Box. When he was on duty at the fire station waiting for calls, we would talk on the phone for hours.

He had two sons, and he claimed he was a single dad. But once, I saw Andre at an outdoor mall in Los Angeles with a woman. I didn't want him to see me, so I didn't do anything to bring any attention to myself. I just hid and watched them. I texted him later and he told me the woman was his sons' mother; he never referred to her as his wife or girlfriend. It wasn't my business and I left it alone out of respect for him and her.

Desperately trying to hustle anything other than ass, I had my bulldog Kina impregnated and she needed check ups. Kina was expecting 7 puppies. Andre agreed to take us to the vet which was almost a six hour round trip event. During the ride, we listened to music; I played with the dog and Andre took several business calls. I felt like the wifey for the first time in my life, riding shotgun in his SUV. I enjoyed Andre taking me to that very important appointment, spending that time with him. I realized that Andre liked me even when I was not dressed up fully as a girl.

He was always happy to see me, and he never told me how to dress or how to be. He didn't attempt to control me or place demands on me like so many other men would. He even surprised me once when he came over my house in his fireman gear. That was very special. Andre always listened to me and looked me in the eyes, and he didn't mind doing things for me. I told him often that I was surprised he would allow himself to get so heavily involved with someone like myself. I think he was just as surprised. But you never know where you can find love or true companionship.

I realized I liked Andre because he represented to me what I desired in my life, a dominant, affectionate father figure. Andre and I honestly never had any bad times,. The best times were when he came over to comfort me during dark times. I had lost two transgender friends, Muffin and Kiwi. Then, a few months later, a male friend Robert was murdered in his home, and then his murderer was himself murdered in LA County Jail. We set Robert's ashes free in the ocean; it was a beautiful service. Shortly after that, the first guy I ever was obsessed with and fell in love with, Yusuf, my Muslim friend, committed suicide.

Months went by, and I didn't give Kina the attention she needed while pregnant. All of Kina's puppies died except one. I named him Miracle. I was so disappointed; I was looking forward to that cash, then my heart broke when she passed away, the second time in my life I grieved losing a pet. Andre was there for me throughout those dark times. The hormones I was taking were making me extremely dramatic and emotional, and I allowed myself to open up and be vulnerable. I remember we laid up in my bed for, like, three hours; no sex, just cuddling and kissing. He made me feel normal and not just like some piece of meat. At this point, money was no longer involved; he wasn't ashamed of me and he also genuinely liked me. The hormones accomplished what was needed, me getting in touch with my feminine side.

I was involved for a couple of years with Andre, but it ended because I wanted more attention and Andre wouldn't give it to me. I think I scared him. I had a hard time controlling my temper tantrums when I didn't get what I wanted from a man, which was more attention. Andre was not about to turn a ho into a housewife, so he said. He would often remind me that it wouldn't work, and that I was just a jump off.

I eventually moved to Culver City and had not spoken to him in a while. He decided to come over to my new apartment to get a massage from me, and he paid me for it. I pointed out that I lived across from a massage parlor, and that I often saw men going in and out of the parlor. A couple of weeks later, I see his truck and him getting out of it to go inside the massage place. I was upset he would do this in front of my home and support these other bitches.

I ran out of my apartment and put a pair of my g-strings on his antenna to let him know he had been spotted. Later when we talked, he denied it, but I knew he was lying. I realized where I had got my temper from; I was like my mom. She hated cheaters, once confessing to me that she shot at my dad when she found out he was cheating on her.

As a result of dating Andre I realized clients were just looking to be entertained, and once they get bored with you, or especially if you get too demanding, they move on. But I would do it all over again. I liked how he made me feel; he was in my life during an extremely important time.

I often think about Andre. I recently googled his name to find out what's going on in his life. He is still putting out fires and saving lives. I never had any pictures of him while we were together, but I was able to pull one off the internet. Andre still has the same phone number, so I texted him and told him I was living in NYC and starting my writing career. I told him that I was writing about our time together. He ignored me, like they all do. I miss the affection he used to give me, and I wish he were lying in bed with me right now.

No one could have told me that walking the streets I would have met such a gentleman and that I would fall in love. As a sex worker, I had closed my heart off and felt unworthy of love. Andre came into my life and ignited a fire in my heart,; he brought out feelings inside me that I didn't know existed. And no, he never said he loved me, but he did show me that he cared for me.

Tasha really started getting out of hand over the years and out of control, she started speaking her mind too much, and she started becoming a real bold bitch. The hormones gave Tasha a false sense of confidence, plus intense feelings of jealousy, envy, and insecurity started to develop. I had become more competitive and the likable personality that once resided in me started to disappear. Tasha's personality was more dominant. My feelings toward men forever changed. From crying, hot flashes, and becoming even more paranoid, it was just too much to bear.

Tasha was driving me crazy and scaring me at the same time. It was like she didn't understand the rules for dealing with these men anymore and didn't want to play by them! The vengeance reared its head, realizing the amount of emotional energy that was draining me because of Tasha. I now needed to sit back and take stock of my life before I got hurt or hurt someone. I had become extremely vulgar and wanted to offend others because I was angry. I was full of rage, feeling so rejected and unloved so I felt like I didn't have to play by societal rules.

It became normal to me to act out throughout out my 20s. There is no one way for someone to deal with being hurt and dealing with trauma or abuse. It became normal to me, but I knew it wasn't how I should be treating myself, because I had been raised better. My core values from birth that my mother had instilled within me remained and became dominant once again. I also discovered along the way no matter what you do to yourself physically to make yourself more attractive, it's kind of pointless, because then people are only attracted to the image you're presenting; They don't like you, they like what you have to offer. I had a lot of stories inside me that I felt were very valuable, that should be told. I decided I would write and start a new hustle in my life. If I created Tasha, I could create anything. It was either suicide or try and find a new way to deal with mental anguish on top of mental anguish, with a side of misery.

After being involved with the seedier side of human nature, up-close and personal, I am now living with stories that could last several lifetimes. I realized it could make for good entertainment.

The dedicated work I performed over the years was more like I was playing the role of therapist, having to sit and listen to others' feelings, thoughts, wishes, and needs. I became extremely over-analytical, having to assess individuals. The stories of abuse, neglect, incest, overwhelmed me. I just wanted to escape the underground world where I had been so consumed for 10 years.

I was getting older and didn't want my life to end as just a sex worker, there are many facets to me and I felt it was time I explored other aspects of my identity rather than keep objectifying myself as a piece of ass. I endured years of self-inflicted dehumanization that for a while I enjoyed and thought was acceptable.

I understood men; it wasn't that they didn't like me, they didn't know how to approach individuals like me in public, were too insecure to do so and were just embarrassed. It was easier in private for them to pay for my attention and to just get right to the point. I knew I was smarter than hustling sex; I had just got spoiled and lazy. There was no longer a need for me to scream for men's attention the way I did when younger. I had finally grown up! The world's oldest profession has become a memory. I'm grateful I allowed myself to go on that journey and that I made it out alive. Now I am playing the role of a writer and drawing from years of hustling and playing in the streets, and I'm feeling proud of myself.

LESSON LEARNED
Danielle

It's counter-intuitive, to fight against the reign of your body when it's in the throes of passion, even if the passion is documented on film. If you're one of the lucky ones that can drown out the cameras, the bright lights, the camera crew, the deafening silence that seems to envelop the sound of your pounding heart and your heavy breathing, in the back of your mind, you still have to fight against the urge, the ravaging, screaming, pounding urge, to shut your legs tight. Snap, quick, clicking like two shells just grazing their edges.

I never smell the ocean when I cum, still I think of oysters.

It was S who told me first: Never close your legs when you're coming, the camera can't see anything.

It had never dawned on me that the camera was the eye that I was playing for, the giant wide-open eye that was the observing my every move.

S was the first person I had met when I started doing porn. At that time, she was a small legend, part of duo that was revolutionizing the way that LGBTQ folks viewed porn. None of this mattered to me, when my girlfriend at the time pointed her out at a dance party, and said, "If you want to make porn, that's who you talk to."

I ran up to S. I was drunk.

"I want to be in your films," I screamed. Probably loudly. I had never been so sure of anything in my life. Later, she would describe the situation as the easiest casting recruitment she ever had to do.

In my real life, when I fucked who I wanted, I would snap my legs shut. The moment of breaking up and never wanting to come undone, unwrapped from my partner, the easiest way was to snap shut my legs. Weave them tightly together, using all my strength, fighting the sweat, just to stay there a bit longer. My legs are strong from ten years of high school athletics and active gym routine.

This is counter-intuitive, yet I remember, in the midst of my performance, because that is what it is, a performance, that the camera's eye, the audience's wide stance on the edge of their seats, does not care about the strength of my upper thighs and my automatic response not to disentangle from my partner.

Even if the sex is just for work.

Still, I remembered with every turn of my body and every turn of the camera, never shut my legs. Always open towards the camera.

Always open towards the camera. Always open for the camera.

Mr. C wasn't the creepy kind of porn director, not that I had the pleasure of meeting too many directors for my judgment to be completely accurate. I think that my general alt appearance in the mainstream porn world, mixed with my brash art form at the moment of no return, took charge of the situation for no bullshit.

Or maybe I was just lucky.

The room was small, in the upstairs part of a large Porn Valley mansion, the type that seem to only be constructed for the purpose of shooting films. No one actually lived in these replications of Home & Beauty commercials, the rooms were furnished completely out of expensive department catalogs. No one real lived liked this, only the make believe students who were always home alone, the new fresh-faced real estate agents, and the tired babysitters.

I once was all of them. Never at the same time.

The room was unfurnished, aside from a large, unmarked bed, fitted with feminine sheets that were neither bright nor frumpy. Mr. C wanted slightly memorable but not overpowering, pretty but not breathtaking. The large bed faced a wall of mirrors, floor to ceiling, that hid a very large and sadly empty closet. These mirrors forgave nothing but flourished only the sense that this was make believe. We could see everything, her and I, as we rolled around on the bed.

This house was not made for the normal folks.

"Whatever you do, do not look in the camera," Mr. C laughed. "If you look in the camera, we will have to reshoot everything, from the beginning."

Spending an entire day rolling around in bed didn't sound half bad, but really, I just wanted to get back to my friend's house with his big yellow Lab and then eat Thai food alone.

The big eyes of the cameras were making me sweat.

We laughed, her and I.

"No looking at the cameras, promise," we said.

The mirrors mocked our promise. How could we not look at ourselves, our egos glaring at us as we performed as best as we could, while the crew stood in front of the unforgiving closet, their back sides reflected back to us as our front sides were captured on film.

We were the meta in creation of porn. An endless mirror of clothed turned into unclothed back into clothed. All for the camera.

It was easy to not look at the cameras, those eyes blinked silently at me, and I had practiced blinking them away.

The mirrors were different, they laughed at my body, at my movements, at my every physical choice.

My hard choice was to not let the mirrors taunt me. I just tried to not look. It was better that way.

NO MATTER HOW HARD YOU FUCK, IT'S ALMOST VALENTINE'S DAY
Sailor

It's the night before Valentine's Day. A dull, cold night and I'm in bed, no bookings and no callers. I'm almost 100% certain I have a bag of gummy bears somewhere. I'll be eating them soon and watching something stupid on television, while half reading a book and a few magazines.

The phone rings and I look at the number. It's a string of numbers, foreign. This is normal for me. I sit up because that's the best way for me to answer in my lowest register.

"Hello," I all but growl, using my hardcore-gay-porn-angry-furrowed-brow voice reserved for unknown callers. I don't quite understand why, but it works.

"Hallo, am I speaking to Say-Luh?" (only they used my actual name).

The string of numbers and the accent click: it's Johannesburg. It's bad, I know that right away.

A lady's voice tells me she is a hospice nurse and that my Mom had just passed. She talks to me for a few minutes and then everything goes still. All of it rushes to the surface and then bleeds away. I pull the covers up and I want to say I am thinking, feeling, but I'm not. I am blank, instantly the opposite of full.

One thought popped up: "Long night ahead!"

How long I lay there, I do not know, not moving, five minutes or twenty. The phone rings with another unknown number and it is not yet 11 pm. It's not yet Valentine's Day here in America, in NYC. But it was Valentine's Day for Mom in Johannesburg, and she died tomorrow on that day with her broken heart. But that day is not yet here.

"Hi ... Sailor?" It's a client, a new one therefore a question mark inside parenthesis (?) in his voice. I listen and I don't. "... just got to my hotel," he stated, "on Wall Street." Am I available for an hour? He needs to get laid, has an early meeting.

I don't skip a beat.

"Yeah, I am," and I scurry to get up and get out, put on a jock and a cock ring - not in that order. A quick topical wipe of my asshole, in case he wants me to sit on his face for a minute or two, brush my teeth, and I'm out the door.

I navigate the way you do when you drive home and can't remember the journey. It's drizzly as I exit the A train. I wanna get really fucked up, that's what I know, I got that bounce, fast steps. My head is silent somehow; my chest is beating hard.

I arrive at the hotel, I am vibrating and flushed one moment and feel nothing in the next one. I go up, I knock on his hotel room door and guess what?

Baby Huey answers the door. A big, pink, flushed, ginger, smiling man fresh from a shower and hopefully a thorough clean out, with a towel wrapped around his big belly, big and firm. He towers over me, I'm 5'7", he's over 6'3" and has a good 150 pounds on me but that is a blessing, an exhausting blessing. You have to work hard to hold on and into the big ones. I call it going little green monkey on 'em. You get the guy on his tummy pull him to the edge of the bed, hold on to what ever you can, man boobs work well, and attach yourself with the force of the jungle.

We chat. He tells me he's a doctor from Baltimore, here for a conference. I might look crazy. Not sure. He asks me if I am "okay" a couple of times.

"Me, never better, baby, let's do this."

We get on the bed, I can tell he wants to get down to business quickly, we do, and we do it.

While we are fucking, for a moment, I bob back into myself, a buoy in my own black ocean. I am drowning. No, I am not drowning, I am bobbing. He grunts, it's hard work holding him down; my big boy. My thoughts are becoming clear again, the rhythm is bringing them back. I want to say, right into his face, sweating, red cheeked, and pleasant: I want to look straight at him and say "My mommy died." I don't say it out loud, instead I weave it into my rhythm: my mummy is dead, my mummy is dead, my mummy is dead...

He cums fast, I don't cum at all and I don't care.

I roll off of him, sweaty ploop, we pant, and pant on the bed side by side, my feet reach just to his shins.

My head is hurting now, a pain behind my eyes is forming. I fight the urge to say it out loud: "My mother just died, just now, far away, in a bed at a hospice... alone." I want to add this, "And you just saved my life because I don't know what I was going to do to get through tonight".

But, I don't.

And now, I'm tired, and I wash up and dress, and function with no connection to touch or surface, everything just happens, he gives me my wad of cash and I roll it and shove it in my front pocket, I enjoy the stuffed feeling of a large amount of cash close to me. I know when I reach the end of this ritual, it's real, it has happened and when I exit the elevator and walk through the plush lobby and out of the doors into the night streets. It is Valentine's Day here in America now and that means my mommy is dead everywhere and that the hearts we couldn't exchange in our ridiculous misconnections over thirty years do not matter now.

The drizzle has ceased and NYC is slick and perfect, quiet and soft. I seem to float into a taxi. It glides without friction. The driver mumbles into his phone, it's all a whirr. Lights are streaking around me. I am navigating on my own in this city. You must, must have a talent for loneliness to be a sex worker; you must be able to understand loneliness' driving force.

My mother and I, Jesus, it was always difficult, she had a hard, hard life. I was yanked from her at 10. We never found a way back to each other. I had hoped she would one day see this city. As I near home in the taxi, I know I will sleep, I just know I will. My mother and I, we were so lonely for each other, and in missing each other we formed some understanding. This city, this work sometimes brings people into contact for brief moments of getting something you may desperately need just then. We all are our true selves here when we function alone.

NAILED UP
Dominick

"Oh, it doesn't matter — you'll be nailed up just like Jesus by time you're thirty-three."

Though it sounds improbable when you say it out loud, it was one of those unarticulated personal myths I'd repeat to myself in my head over and over to justify my choices. The story gained credibility over years of repetition, even though, or perhaps because, I'm what the Church calls "fallen away." Though the Catholic Church of my youth had weak currents of Seventies Liberation Theology running through it—I distinctly remember a nun with a guitar leading Catechism class in an awkward rendition of Michael, Row the Boat Ashore—the hierarchy was still entrenched in Old-World damnation. This was confusing.

My true disaffection with the Church began at the age of thirteen, on the occasion of my first confession:

Me: "Bless me Father, for I have sinned."

(Silence)

The priest, whispering impatiently: "Well, what are your sins?"

I was appalled by his question. Maybe I wasn't paying attention in class, but I fully expected that the priest would be able to tell me what my sins were, divining them through the stamped metal screen. Where's the magic in telling? Why bother with this ornate wooden booth?

I couldn't even think of any good sins I'd committed, honestly (cursing?), so if he couldn't tell me what was wrong, what good was he? I walked out of the booth, leaving that presumptuous priest hanging, and walked straight home in sullen disillusionment, never to return to the Catholics (at least in body). I told my parents I wouldn't be returning to Catechism and they honored my decision.

Not only was I rebellious, I was also a pretty narcissistic adolescent boy—not that uncommon, but this trait flourished under my family's coddling. I was the first-born son in a generation of an Italian immigrant family that held on to old-world values through the social upheavals of the seventies. My immediate family may have looked young and hip, but we were pretty traditional— Seventies outfits and hairstyles, Fifties moral code and social order. I was treated like the little prince of the household, lavished with affection and indulgences, and favored by my grandma with extra cookies. I had a seat at the big dining room table for Sunday dinners with the extended family, while my younger brother and cousins were banished to the dreaded kid's table, a folding thing in the alcove.

Despite privileged status within my extended family, out in the wider world, I became dissociative. I was awkward, disconnected, and generally unimpressed by my flat, suburban Long Island surroundings. I was out of touch with my male peers. I was barely able to form friendships, except with other narcissistic loners. I was incapable of developing the sense of cooperation and common purpose required for team sports (track was the only sport in which I participated, as a sprinter and a jumper). I was overly sensitive, and generally misunderstood. These three factors—my early rebellion against the Church, for which I felt I would surely be punished; my highly developed narcissism; the general condition of alienation—contributed to my identification with the nailed-up body of Jesus. Maybe there was a touch of masochism in there, too.

My inner self whispered this fate for so long and so convincingly that I burned through my twenties with an abandon masking superstitious fatalism; my timeline was predetermined. I chain-smoked unfiltered cigarettes. I adapted the pose of a louche, a dissolute, a drinking and travel companion to an aristocratic, alcoholic British decorator. He was an Italophile, a lover of all things Italian: villas, statues, food, men. He harbored a romantic obsession for me that I responded to with increasing cruelty. I travelled all over Europe with this man, who himself looked like a pope. We visiting palaces, fabulous gardens, and splendid ruins, all settings in which, we agreed, I belonged.

After his addiction, and heartbreak in the face of my cruelty, put the decorator in a bronze urn, I embarked on my thirties with a nice fat inheritance. My alcoholic Sugar Daddy was dead, and I was free to live on my own terms. But it turns out that I'd been getting high for so long, just to put up with the drunken old man, that I'd cultivated addictions of my own. I graduated from cocktail companion to roached-out stoner to dope sniffer within a year. I sensed my timeline winding down, and would occasionally check my palms for stigmata.

When I turned thirty-four, I found that I wasn't dead, just really impaired and more susceptible than ever to fractured religious destruction myths. I could no longer count on myself or the decorator or his dwindling money for answers—or questions, for that matter. I fashioned my own nails out of pure white powder, the purest you could find in New York, procured by a South American boyfriend. I drove them into my head instead of my hands. I didn't know where I was going, but in my delusional fugue state, Thor Heyerdahl's voiceover told me that there was Trans-Atlantic trade between South America and North Africa via the Canary Current; that traders in reed boats navigated the current, and that's how it is they found cocaine in the mummies buried inside pyramids. So I was sniffing the pure white powder of the ancient pharaohs.

After just a few months of the white powder trans-Atlantic reed boat up the Nile adventure ride, I was hung up, mouth gaping open, but no words issuing forth, dumbstruck, my neural network fried, nothing crossing those synapses, like bridges burned. This proved to be a blessing, since I could only listen, possibly for the first time in my life. I landed in a recovery program, and have found that each addictive substance found in my own mummified body—tobacco, cocktails, cannabis, dope, white powder—had its own intrinsic half-life, like radioactive isotopes. Each decays at a specific rate, eventually reaching acceptable background levels. Every day since has been a resurrection (I know, we're scrambling time and place and burial myths,)

There are depictions of Jesus coasting out of his crumpled body, or out of the cave, and into the heavenly light. But this is my resurrection, and I won't be encumbered by any timeworn mythologies any longer. I can be whatever I want in my resurrection, and no dead celebrity savior is going to tell me otherwise. As long as there is light. A sobered up man in an impaired world, a sacred prostitute, a corporate executive, a road warrior, a gay hobo, a Pagan. I can bend scripture until it fits. It's been mis-translated for centuries by men with forked tongues, so maybe I'm forking it back into shape. I like Mark 12:31, for instance: "Love thy neighbor." I've loved as many of them as I can, and now thanks to GPS-enabled cruising apps and the satellite array encircling the earth, constantly transmitting signals into my pocket, I will love more.

This formative myth of the Catholic faith ensnared me in its thorny, longhaired clutches, and I've spent a lifetime running from it. Jesus was a rambler and how I have rambled. Jesus loved his fellow men, and I have too, as many of them as I could.

My table is full of hot apostles. Jesus washed the feet of a prostitute and so have I, every time I shower. It was a story made great through years of repetition, my own Catechism, and it ran my life, until it didn't, and this is heaven. It was a great story I told, because I have bent time, space, geography, history, science, the social order, reason, morality, and judgment to make it fit. Matthew 28:6: He is not here; he has risen.

NO RESTRICTIONS
Dee Dee Behind

My very first session with a client with severe disabilities was while I was working as a professional dominatrix on the third floor of a dungeon in an elevator-less building. In addition to the logistical nightmare of getting a man in a motorized wheelchair onto four hours of public transportation and then up three flights of stairs, how, exactly, was I to tie up someone who was already completely physically immobile?

Paul, a man in his fifties with a degenerative condition that affected his nervous system, wrote a letter, a snail mail letter, to the listed P.O. box of the dungeon, explaining his deep and unrelenting desire to be whipped. This, he said, had captured his imagination ever since our dungeon was featured on a silly public access television show that highlights the "wild and offbeat" places of my hometown of Chicago.

Paul explained in his nearly illegible and deliberate handwriting his concern that his parents, still his primary caregivers despite his own age and independence, might think he was being abused by his attendants should they find marks or bruises on his body. He was deeply ashamed to admit that this had happened in the past after he managed to pinch his own genitals for sexual pleasure until he left deep purple bruises. The suspected attendant had been fired and was barely spared criminal charges, and Paul would never live down the regret he felt for the trouble he caused her.

But to come clean and discuss desire, particularly his pleasure of pain, was not an option for him. It was one thing to have erections during sponge baths, but a penchant for masochism would have been too much for those who cared for him. Paul was surrounded by people whom he depended on, not just for a lifeline to all things physically beyond the reach of his crippled body, but also for their emotional ties to him created by his own helplessness. His helplessness was his survival.

As a sex worker, I can imagine that if the source of those bruises were traced back to me, the consequences would be devastating. It freaks me out right now, just thinking about it. I imagine how I might explain consent to reporters at my courthouse interview while standing trial for felony sexual abuse of the helplessly disabled. How could consent exist in such a lop-sided power dynamic? To believe that this was a consensual sexual experience would mean to concede to the sexual autonomy of a man who cannot feed or clothe himself. But here was the man's desires, in black smudgy ink, an eloquent request he preferred to submit to me in writing, because, as the letter continued to explain, his ability to speak is also severely impaired and therefore he is unable to express himself with speech. Great. I imagined burning in hell in fishnets.

After Paul arrived in his motorized wheelchair, and a long battle to get him up the stairs in the chair failed, I chained up the chair with my bicycle lock to the steel handles of our downstairs lobby doors, while the house wrestling domme carried him up the three flights of stairs to the dungeon. After strapping him to a wheeling gurney we kept as a medical prop in the "doctor's office," I carefully undressed him. I was terrified I was going to hurt him. The irony.

Paul's body was twisted and unwieldy, his skin a pasty white. His bony apple-shaped ribcage was topped with a huge lopsided head, giving it the illusion of growing out of his shoulder. His face was frozen in an insane smile. I could not tell if he was incredibly happy or horribly contorted. I peeled down his pants to discover, to my 19-year-old only-a-year-in-the-biz shock, a raging hard penis, prominent and quite impressive in size. It stuck straight out of the dark recess of his lap, a lap permanently frozen in a sitting position.

He made little encouraging snorting noises as I admonished him for being a horny little slut—so encouraging in fact, that I raised my hand in a threatening gesture as if I were going to slap his cock in punishment for his digressions. When I did this, Paul went wild. His eyes grew huge and he spasmed with excitement, making these crazy disturbing honking noises that emanated deep from inside his face. The entire session was one long negotiation of me being terrified I was hurting him, and him getting incredibly turned on, and then me becoming a little less terrified, and on and on it went. In the end, he came multiple times with only the stimulation of a riding crop whipping his cock—the mark of a true masochist.

After hauling wheelchairs up and down flights of stairs more than once in the past 15 years of being a sex worker, I think about the barriers to sexual pleasure people who are disabled face all the time, both the physical and the social. In addition to the isolation people with disabilities face, stemming from their exclusion from physical spaces and communities designed for able-bodied adults only, many social situations prohibit people with disabilities from fully participating in adulthood. The world continues to shift and change around this, but sexuality seems the exemption.

However, despite being shielded most of their lives from the topic of sexuality, no disabled client has ever contacted me with the naïvete about sex that is portrayed in Hollywood versions of disability. Portrayals of sexuality of the disabled as innocent assuage our discomfort around the topic of different bodies and queerness. The reason they "feel good" is because they confront what disturbs us about the desires of the non-desirable. Their sexuality is transformed into something normative and comfortable only if we recast the disabled as children, and the hookers as saints.

A few years ago, I received an email from Justin, a 22-year-old virgin. He explained he was a person with a disease that made him unable to use his muscles and therefore needed a wheelchair, constant care, and an attendant who was typing the very email that I was presently reading. He was a virgin, and could I help him? He had the blessing of his attendant, but not his disapproving parents, who still spoke to him in a baby voice. Could I accommodate the unusual situation?

I squinted to examine the picture attached to the email, a face propped up with pillows inside a huge motorized chair that swallowed his tiny frame. The idea of taking something—anything—from him made me feel uncomfortable.

I knew that stigmatization of disability was the real barrier to Justin's sexual satisfaction, not his inability to use his limbs. By recognizing my own feelings of discomfort as an acculturation to infantilize Justin, and responding to him instead as the horny 22-year-old he was, I was trying to practice direct resistance to the everyday sexual oppressions and stigmas that all queer-bodied people face. Part of why I love being a sex worker is because I am part of a revolution to liberate the world from shame, heteronormativity, and social isolation.

But, at the same time, I grew up on this planet the same as everyone else. I try to unpack my privilege, and sometimes I fall short: I hate my girl body, I "yuck" someone's "yum," or I am too scared to touch twisted limbs. Even though I'm scared, I keep chipping away at my own shit, going deeper and deeper into that world of Balls-Out Whore Fantastica, where everyone wears leopard print spandex and speaks openly and curiously about shocking topics at the dinner table. This is how we get that way, that place where the shocking is normal. Among other things, it is one of the sex worker super powers that makes us soldiers in this revolution; we pull it together and pretend someone didn't just scare the shit out of us with their drunken violence, that they didn't just shit in our hand, or they didn't deeply offend us with a stigmatizing back-handed compliment mid-fellatio. Or, at the very least, that all these things happened, but didn't bother us one bit.

I didn't offer Justin any special accommodation except to waive my extra $100 travel fee. Is this a practice that balances helpful but not patronizing? To respect his sexuality by treating him like any other man, even if that means shaking him down for all he's got? Is charging full price an act of solidarity? Or am I risking blowing his cover, because honestly, this man has no job, and how the hell can he hide a $300 bank account withdrawal? Did Justin feel like he had a political ally in this sex worker, someone who could provide comfort in his sexual normalcy, as I do for all of my clients? Or am I just a blood-sucking whore to him too? After all, he also grew up on the same planet as everyone else.

He and his attendant conspired to use the attendant's father's house while he was away on vacation, making the appointment an all-day production and a complex web of deceit for both of them. For me, it was a 2 pm outcall. I borrowed the car of a friend, another sex worker.

"I'm leaving now!" I yelled, picking up the keys from her foyer table. My friend in her computer room-slash-home office-slash-webcamming stage didn't answer. "Going to take a crippled man's vir-gin-it-yyyy," I sing-songed, pausing for an answer from down the hall.

"Have fun," she said, without even directing her voice towards the door to the hallway.

"You're so amazing," said a voice off the foyer, just as I was opening the front door. I turned and it was my friend's roommate. Leaning against the kitchen counter with a cup of tea in both hands, she cocked her head and made a face. I know this face. It's the "sex work is a public service" face. It's the "you are such a good person... and I could never do what you do" face. For the first time since booking this session, I felt gross. I wanted to scratch her eyes out.

I drove around a deserted subdivision looking for the address number along rows of identical looking houses. I found the house because it was the only one with a car in the driveway -- an ancient grey minivan covered in special designation stickers, yellow warnings on all sides, and bulky door modifications, sitting in all its disabled obviousness in the driveway.

When I knocked on the door, I was surprised to find that the attendant, a profession usually reserved for women, was instead a handsome young frat boy about Justin's age. He explained that Justin wanted to skip through the undignified aspect of making me wait the 30 minutes it took to get him from clothed in a wheelchair to naked in bed, so they did it already. Justin was waiting in the bedroom, and he hoped I wasn't freaked out. "I'm not," I lied.

In a whisper, the attendant expressed his ambivalence about helping Justin get laid, since he could lose his job, or possibly worse. He was visibly distraught describing how no one around him took Justin seriously as a young man, not just censoring him from the world of adults, but also disallowing him the right to grow up.

He feared Justin's parents were emotionally invested in keeping Justin five-years-old. He was afraid that by denying Justin his desire to get finally get laid, he would be just like the parents. So he consented to help, even though he really didn't want to.

After some consoling and reassurance, I was led to the doors of the bedroom. I slipped though the double doors alone, into the dark, carpeted chamber. The bed consumed the entire room. At first I didn't see him, his small body covered in folds of sheets. But my eyes adjusted, and from the doorway, I could make out the side of his face, his hair, a shoulder, all completely still.

"Justin?" I said, into the quiet.

Without moving or laying eyes on me, he bellowed, "Hello there, sexy!"

My session with Justin was unremarkable in that when it came right down to it, Justin was like any other man who is 22 and still a virgin—wide eyed and easy to impress. Justin was mature, funny and self-deprecating, and I enjoyed his company, careful to not lay the hustle on too thick, lest he mistake my desire to make him feel good for the paternalism that is suspiciously heaped onto people with disabilities. Able-bodied men, hilariously enough, have no such "bullshit meter" for praise.

I imagine Justin had a great time, but I doubt he could care less about the intersecting politics of disability and sex work. He was, after all, just wanting to get laid out of the arrangement, and wasn't really interested in joining a whore revolution. And I, for all my radical political beliefs, am in this game to get paid. I like to think something is traded in those exchanges besides sex and money, but you never really know. I know that I made some kind of impression on Justin, because I got an email from him a week later. Thanks for the good time, he said, but I am not his type. Did I have a friend? Someone blonde perhaps, with big breasts?

ARISTOCRAT
Sur Madam

I think about three things when I begin my workday as a dog walker: the weather, a possible emergency trip to the vet, and raising my rates. Please note that I did not mention thinking about a stranger on the street offering to pay me to engage in his extreme, fetishistic desires, but that is how I got my start in sex work.

It was an August afternoon, and I was walking two devastatingly adorable Pug/Brussel Griffon mutts. One of the pups paused to eliminate on the curb. As I bent over to pick it up, I heard a calm, soft voice. "Those dogs are so cute. They are so lucky to be walked by such a Goddess. May I call you Goddess?" To be honest, I don't care for it, but since I don't absolutely hate it, I let it go. "Eh, sure", I replied, making sure to took as disinterested as possible. He didn't acknowledge my look and continued to speak, giving me many compliments. Then the conversation turned graphic. Not graphic in the way I was accustomed to being spoken to on the street. No, none of that "you got a fat ass" and "you a dyke cos you ain't had no good dick" talk. I'm talking graphic in a Salò or Pink Flamingos way. I wrote off the man as a weirdo, but I like weirdos, so I continued to listen. His desires didn't bother me, if anything I found them funny. He made an offer that I chose to oblige. I don't know why. Looking back, I believe the tranquility of this voice created a static that prevented me from comprehending what he said. That static gave way to my entry in the trade.

Me: What's your address?
Sissy: 123 Sissy Street apt 4B(itch)

First Date
             I was standing outside his place on Sissy Street
feeling nauseous. My nerves were a wreck. I've never done
anything this extreme before. The proposal was disgusting and
vile, two concepts that I very much enjoy, but I didn't know this
guy. I didn't know what he was capable of. He made this
proposal on the street in broad daylight, so he clearly had a lot of
testicular fortitude. The fact that he asked me, even offered to
pay me, to do what I was about to do should have sounded all
alarms. However, I tend to go deaf at the hint of danger.
             He buzzed me in. I walked up the four floors in 90
degree weather. I stopped midway up the last floor to catch my
breath. I hate the idea of people witnessing how terribly out of
shape I am. When I reached the top of the stairs, I texted my
brother with Sissy's information: name, address, telephone
number, names of affiliates, and even the name of his mother—a
self help guru.
             The door was slightly ajar. I pushed it open and saw
him. A husky, sunburnt man lying naked atop plastic bags, with a
makeshift toilet covering his face. It was a white wastebasket
with a white toilet seat covering the top. He had cut a hole in the
side to fit his head. I shook my head, thought, "White people are
so fucking crazy," and put down my bag. I saw my money on the
marble mantle. Six fifty dollars bills just as I demanded. All was
silent except for the sound of him playing with his small, cut
penis. His balls were being asphyxiated by a leather cuff.
             My stomach cramped, and that was my signal. I peered
into the toilet to see him with his eyes shut and mouth wide
open. I took off my pants, sat, and let go. He let out a deep
moan, and his once limp dick quickly rose. It was like watching a
time lapse video of a growing flower. When I was done, I
hopped off the toilet and ran to the bathroom to clean myself. I
returned to him still laying there, still playing with himself, still
eating. He was a quiet eater. I remember nodding in

appreciation as I walked out the door without saying anything to him.

Lunchtime
A few months went by before I saw him again. I managed to find more toilet slaves and pick up a few tricks in the meantime. The work swelled my ego and bank account. I was getting paid to have rich White men eat my shit. Doing one of the most basic and essential bodily functions was paying my rent. The work also made me very self conscious about how my stool looked, so I made small changes to my diet. I ate more fibrous foods and began juicing beets, kale, and spinach. The fellas loved chewing my purple and green gems. I researched how to make my poop smell better or not at all. The search proved pointless since I learned that part of the appeal was the aromatherapy.

We ran into each other one fall afternoon. I took a sudden interest in The Village Voice, grabbed a paper, and walked around the corner to an alley. He slowly approached me, tilted his head, and batted his lashes like a preteen girl trying to be sexy and began to explain himself: "Hi Goddess. I'm sorry I haven't called. I got really sick after my first meal, so I decided to lay off for a bit. I'm ready now. I would really like for your shit to be a part of my diet. You can just come over to my place, take a dump, and leave laughing at the thought of this sissy White boy eating your shit. I want to lick your asshole clean, Goddess. You can fart in my mouth while I'm worshipping your beautiful ass."

I didn't challenge his claim to being sick. After all, he did eat a bunch of shit. Part of me was curious if he saw other Toilet Mistresses, just as I was seeing other Toilet Slaves. I didn't care enough to ask. In fact, I didn't know what to say, so I responded by farting. I wanted to laugh hysterically; it took everything in me to 1) feel comfortable farting in public—it was louder than I expected it to be, and 2) keep a straight, stern face. Before I could think of something clever, sexy, and demanding to say, he bit his lip and said, "Thank you for letting me be in the presence of your fart, Goddess. I just wish I was kneeling down behind you so you could have farted in my face."

Internally, I was squealing and giggling. That shit was rich, too fucking rich. I still couldn't speak, so I spat in his face. Sissy dropped to his knees and asked if he could lick my sneakers. I was totally unbothered by that point. I was fine with the fart and spitting, but having someone at my feet in public made me uncomfortable. I told him to get this White, shit eating, baby dick having, sorry ass up and listen. I gave him a price and told him I'd be in touch. That was a lie. I didn't have to be in touch, I knew he'd contact me within the next few days. Sure as shit, I got a text message two days later:

> Sissy: Hi Goddess.
> Me: Hello Sissy.
> Sissy: I'm very hungry. May I please be fed today, Mistress?
> Sissy: I'll be home until 5 pm.
> Sissy: Please GODDESS???
> Me: I'll consider you.
> Sissy: Yes Mistress.

I didn't think I would see him that day because it was almost 3:30 pm and I didn't urge. I just finished playing with a dog, so I went to the bathroom to freshen up and pee before the commute home. The slightest push and I ended up taking a huge dump. The thing just snuck up on me. I got up to examine the goods. God damn, I should consider charging by the ounce. There goes lunch, I remember thinking to myself.

The next thought was probably the most genius, the most hilarious, the most abhorrent thought I had to date. I went to the kitchen and grabbed two slices of twelve grain bread, snatched a poop bag off the dog's leash and went back to the bathroom. With one piece of bread in my left hand, I sheathed my right with the poop bag, just as I would when picking up after a dog. I kicked up the seat, reached into the toilet, and grabbed a big handful of brown mush. I pick up after dogs all the time and it doesn't bother me. However, having a handful of my own warm shit made me violently gag. My mission, however revolting, was too genius to abort so I continued. I smeared the mush evenly on the bread, then went in for a second round. I grabbed one of the solid pieces for texture. I quartered it and placed it atop the mush. I sent Sissy a text when I cleaned up:

Me: Be there in 20.
Sissy: Yes Mistress! Thank you Mistress!! <3

I double wrapped the sandwich, placed it in a brown paper bag, and headed to his house. Once again, he was on the floor with the makeshift toilet on his head. I grabbed and counted my money, then ordered him to get up and dressed. I waited by the door with my arms behind my back. He was obviously confused, but didn't question me. He got dressed and sat on the couch. I went to the kitchen, pour a glass of milk, sliced an apple, and plated his sandwich. He continued to look confused as I put his meal in front of him. "Soup's on," I said. He lifted the bread and examined the sandwich meat. "Oh Goddess," he said. "You're so cruel." As I turned to leave, he asked if I was going to watch him eat it. The thought never crossed my mind. To be honest, I didn't care because he got his shit, and more important, I got my money. However, I couldn't resist my desire for the disgusting, so I took a seat. I sat and watched Sissy eat his special sandwich like it was a fucking BLT. He ate an apple slice and washed it down with milk. I never liked the way a milk and apple snack tasted. I can't imagine the havoc a milk, apple, and feces snack wreaked on the tastebuds. He looked up and told me how the sandwich, now three quarters finished, was hearty and delicious. Then he tilted his head, batted his lashes, and smiled. A fucking shit. Eating. Grin. Time stopped. I took a moment to examine his face. The eyes were dark, but clearly full of joy. His skin was still very red and his smile was, God damn. I never paid close attention to his mouth before, so I didn't know if he had small gaps between every tooth, or had shit stuck between his teeth.

As time resumed, I began to look around at the books and photos in the room. My eyes caught the photo of a woman. She was a beautiful, full figured, cafe au lait colored woman. I knew who she was, the fiancee. Normally, I never had concern for a sissy's vanilla life, but I couldn't help but to think about her. I imagined them kissing, using their tongues. Does she taste my lunch? Does she say anything if she notices something is off? Does she know about his hunger? When he comes home suspiciously late, does she smell his breath instead of smelling his dick? The last thought made me chuckle.

He asked," Do you think it's funny that you have this White boy sissy eating your shit, Mistress?"

"No," I sternly replied, "All White boys should be eating my shit. It isn't comedy, it's your fucking place."

He nodded in agreement, finished his meal, and paused. I began to cringe because I thought he was going to burp. Instead, he thanked me for the filling meal. He never had a special sandwich before, and needed to give his Goddess and extra tribute for the special gift. He grabbed a book off the mantle and pulled out two hundred dollars. "Thank you, Mistress."

Finale

We began having bi-weekly dates. There were more sandwiches, and I came up with two more meals: diarrhea shakes and spaghetti and shitballs. I made him bob for turds in the toilet while shoving a plug in his butt. My rent was getting paid, my student loan balance was decreasing, and I had hilarious stories to tell at parties.

He called me after a three week silence to tell me he was moving. He was getting married and his fiancee wanted to move back home. He had time for one more date with Goddess, and he wanted it to be extra special. He wanted the motherload. My job was to save all my bowel movements for a week and deliver it to his studio. I thought that was impossible and too extreme, even for me, until he named the amount he was willing to pay. Anything was possible and nothing was extreme for that price. He gave me half up front. I had a few surprises in store and needed to pick up a few things. I took off a week of work and stayed at my grandmother's house. I imagined it would be easier to hide a container of shit in a two family house with a deserted garage than it would be in a three bedroom apartment. My diet was chaos. I ate all the right and wrong foods to get things going: highly fibrous cereals, cabbage, Indian food, and laxatives. I had to buy another container after day three.

When our finale date arrived, I ordered him to send a car for me. Can you imagine carrying two container of feces on the train? That would be an interesting conversation with law enforcement. I bound the bins together and put them in a heavy duty Hefty bag. Then I carried it and my bag of supplies to the car myself.

I arrived at his studio to see him in his usual position. He began to speak, probably something along the lines of "thank you, Goddess this" and "sissy White boy that". I couldn't pay attention because I was looking for my money. He had my full consideration when I finished counting. I took a seat and ordered him to lick my grey Converse. As he cleaned, I began to tell him what a good slave he'd been and he was my favorite piggy. Then, I took off my pants and bent over so he could worship my body while I farted in his face. He begged to eat my ass, and I obliged. Last day, you know? He moaned at every moment of flatulence. I bent further down and managed to see his flower growing. Time to get started.

I moved away from him, opened my bag of tricks, and put on my strap-on harness and gloves. Then I pulled out my special gift for him--a pig nose. "Oh Goddess, you're so much fun," he giggled. I emptied one container in front of him then opened and stood by a window. He was commanded to eat, which he began doing very slowly. I opened another window and began circling him, calling him a pig and demanding he made pig noises. The pig began talking with his mouth full and begging me to fuck him. I eased in and began giving him a handjob. I increased my pace then without warning, shoved his head in the shit. He came immediately. I emptied the other container and allowed him a moment to reconstitute. He tenderly spoke about how I was a true Goddess (whatever that means), he loved the way my big black cock (it was purple) felt in his tight White boy ass, then a chorus of thank yous.

I stood back and watched him catch his breath while squeezing handfuls of shit. An overwhelming sense of megalomania took me over. There in front of me was a White, male trust fund fuck, who was paying me handsomely for the honor of consuming my digested meals. I felt like I just did something for every broke motherfucker, every Black motherfucker, every woman.

Round two began. I was not gentle with him this go round. I wanted to get in his guts and really make him squeal like a pig. He didn't ask me to slow down or stop; he just braced himself and kept eating. I shoved his face in the mess and smeared it in his hair. Then, I grabbed a handful and caked his entire face. "You got some color on you now, boy. But you still have a tiny White boy dick". I pulled his mouth open and shoved it full of poop while I pounded. He took his humiliation like a champ. He just moaned and munched away.

He went silent after a few minutes. As I was about to say something, his back curled and brown foamy sludge shot out of his mouth and across the floor. I backed up and began to heave. I turned my back and heard another gag and splatter. I went to an open window, yanked off the gloves, covered my mouth, and closed my eyes tight while I listened to him vomit. I felt the need to still look tough, so I tried to keep my gags as inaudible as possible.

My head was pounding. Small, colorful, blinking dots were all I could see. When I turned around, I saw him on his side, one hand cupping his buttock. It was time to throw in the towel. I got dressed as quickly as possible. There was vomit on my bag, so I shoved the cash in my bra, Metrocard and ID in my pocket, and keys on my belt loop.

I took a final look before I opened the door. He was in the same position, breathing heavily. I couldn't tell if his eyes were open because his head was down and face was caked. My resolve began to dissipate. I wanted him to speak so badly. I didn't want to be Goddess anymore. I wanted to ask if he was okay, if he needed help, but I didn't.

I went to the restroom to make sure I looked and smelled clean. I looked like shit. My eyes were as red as his skin the moment before our date. My skin was dull. Anxiety consumed me and I felt nauseous. I stared in the mirror and tried to force myself to smile, but it proved impossible. I raced to the elevator and watched his doorknob as I pressed the door close button.

ABOUT THE CONTRIBUTORS

ANNA SAINI has lived many lives as a political scientist, radical activist, and multi-media artist. She completed a B.A. and M.A. in Political Science at the University of Toronto and McMaster University respectively. She is passionately dedicated to grassroots community organizing on drug and education policy reform, civil and labor rights, prison abolition, anti-police brutality, and post-colonial feminist liberation. Her work has appeared in *Bitch Magazine*, *Make/Shift Magazine*, the *Dear Sister* anthology, *Feminism for Real*, various journals and her self-published women of color poetry anthology, *Colored Girls*.

BRANDON AGUILAR grew up in Kansas City, Missouri. He has an MFA in painting from the School of the Art Institute of Chicago. He appeared in a number of gay porn titles, such as "Closed Set: Oral Report," directed by Joe Gage and "Christian's 24 Cocks in 24 Hours" by Treasure Island Media. He lives in Brooklyn.

DANIELLE has a long standing love affair with linguistics, which developed in her younger years down south in New Jersey. Since her rise from a young babe into a babe of current years, she wore many hats, from professional cook at a meditation center to photography studio manager. With her tech-savvy understanding of online identities, Danielle spoke publicly on many occasions about the interaction of sex, workers in the industry, and their presence on the internet. Since her arrival to New York City, almost two years ago, she has maintained multiple freelance writing gigs, addressing all things music and photography. When she isn't keeping sexy time hours at her full-time job, Danielle is held captive by her two cats and her love of science, all while finding time to create films with her best friend and determine the exact moment of the singularity's arrival.

DEE DEE BEHIND is a sex worker, mostly. She is new to New York and wants to make friends.

DION P. SCOTT is blessed with audacity and the gifts of determination and courage. He came of age in Hollywood, CA where he explored a career in entertainment as an actor and model by day, booking national commercials and print jobs. Intrigued by the nightlife, he was seduced into moonlighting as a street hustler. He abandoned his entertainment career, learned the tricks of the trade, and became a global traveler, hustling along the way. He is also a devout sports aficionado. Dealing with societal injustices and prejudices towards marginalized groups has led Dion to become a civil rights advocate. He currently lives in NYC, where he is launching his independent screenwriting and producing projects.

DOMINICK is a Brooklyn-born Italian who found his confessional voice as a regular at Dean Johnson's Reading for Filth series. He struggles to recall his twenties, which he spent as the kept boy of a drunken English decorator of some renown. In his thirties he embarked on a career as an escort. He traced a heat map of desire across the greater metropolitan area, which is captured in his escort diary. He retired upon transitioning to a management position at one of New York City's largest real estate interests. Dominick now writes for blog.rentboy.com, offering escorts and clients alike advice drawn from his experience. He's a frequent presence at Red Umbrella Diaries, and has appeared in Dan Savage's podcast and Savage Love column. Several pieces appear in the inaugural issue of *Prose & Lore*, and his story "Dirty Tricks, Happy Endings" appears in the Soft Skull anthology *Johns, Marks, Tricks & Chickenhawks*.

ESSENCE REVEALED is first generation Bajan born &
raised in Boston. She got her BFA at NYU's Tisch School of the
Arts and MA at NYU's Steinhardt School of Education. Her
writing has appeared places such as *Spread Magazine, Corset
Magazine*, BurlesqueBible.com and *21st Century Burlesque*.
She's been published in two anthologies: *Prose & Lore #1 &
Johns, Marks, Tricks & Chicken Hawks*. She now performs &
teaches nationally and internationally both solo and as a member
of Brown Girls Burlesque. Her favorite thing to do besides
reading is to lounge on the beach in Barbados resting up for a
night of calypso dancing.

GERRY VISCO is a writer, photographer, performer,
fashionista, and nightlife personality. She currently writes for
Interview Magazine and *Hyperallergic* and has published
hundreds of article in *New York Press, Out Magazine, The
New York Sun, Edge Media, The Village, Beyond Race, Fit
Yoga, Our Town, West Side Spirit, The Chelsea Clinton News,
New York Blade, Gay City News, Spread Magazine, Columbia
Review*, and the *Adobe Anthology*. Her photography has
appeared in *Interview Magazine, Hyperallergic, New York
Magazine, The Village Voice, One* (art journal in Bulgaria), *The
Daily News*, and *Gawker. The Village Voice* named her
Bravest Nightlife Photographer of 2010 and she was nominated
for a Glam Award as best nightlife writer in 2010 and 2011. Visco
holds a BA in Literature, an MFA in Writing, and an MS in
Journalism from Columbia University. She is currently writing a
memoir about her colorful lie in the gritty glamorous world of
New York City during the 1970s and 1980s. She lives on the
Upper East Side, has a day job, and barely sleeps.

HIMA B. makes documentaries, narratives, experimental films/videos that explore intersections between race, gender, sexual orientation, labor, and economics in relation to women and girls. Born in India and raised in the US, she earned an MFA from Mills College while stripping and being a teaching assistant. She came into filmmaking through the crossroads of her sexuality, sex worker labor organizing, and desire to use the moving image to address social justice issues. Hima directed the following documentaries: *Straight For The Money* (1994) about lesbian and bisexual sex workers; *Coming Out Coming Home* (1996) with four Asian Pacific Islander Families coming to terms with their adult children's homosexuality; and *How Do You Tell Somebody That You're HIV+?* (2010) which follows a day in the life of a young African American woman who struggles to disclose her HIV status to her ex. This last short is part of a ten-part series called *HIV Sisters*, which documents the experiences of women and girls who are infected, impacted, or at risk for the virus. Hima is currently in post-production on her feature documentary, *License to Pimp*, about the choices that three strippers make as their strip clubs engage in illegal labor practices, which result in them becoming de facto brothels. "I Remember Market Street Cinema" is the first memoir Hima has written about her former experiences in the sex industry.
www.HimaB.com
www.LicenseToPimp.com
www.HIVsisters.org

LILY FURY has been writing since she was a little girl, and she wants to thank Meliss5a Petro and Audacia Ray for helping her develop her talent as a writer. She is published in the newly released *Corner Stories*, an anthology of writings by the Washington Heights Corner Project community under the name Naomi Madsen.

MANDY TZ is a white trans woman who enjoys nothing more than telling a heavily tattooed man begging to worship her that she can't hear him cause she has "Ace of Spades" blasting from her speakers. She may seem sensitive from her piece but she's actually an evil, merciless slut devoted to instituting female supremacy. You can contact her for plans of future co-femme world domination at hornyliltz69@gmail.com

NICOLETTE DIXON worked in strip clubs in California in New York from 2003 to 2010. She's been writing, in journals, poems, and damn good love letters, since she was six years old and got brave enough to share some of that writing in public starting at 24 years old. She's passionate about accessible art making, social justice, and finding the best latte in the city. She's honored to have been included in this issue of *Prose & Lore*, and you can find more from her in the upcoming publication *Pros on Parenting.*

REI is an exiting and re-entering disciplinarian based in New York City.

RITA RACHAELS found her road less traveled in New York City.

SAILOR has bartended, waited tables, worked as a freelance prop-stylist, a bathhouse attendant, go-go bear, schoolteacher and house painter. Reared in Johannesburg and Tel Aviv, he is now a "freelancer of the night" or "your average next door beefy furry cub for hire." Being an escort has given Sailor time to spend his days writing and daydreaming. He is working on a collection of poems and non-fiction essays. All major credit cards accepted.

SUR MADAM is a bi-coastal, supervenient Toilet Mistress and pet care provider. She is a five-fold college dropout with seemingly shoddy lifestyle choices, and couldn't be more pleased with herself.

ABOUT THE EDITOR

AUDACIA RAY is the founder and executive director of the Red Umbrella Project. She is a former sex worker who is passionate about supporting people in the sex trades as they tell their stories.

To contribute to *Prose & Lore* or participate in future memoir workshops and other RedUP programs, email Dacia at audaciaray@redumbrellaproject.org or call the RedUP office at 347-927-3867.

ABOUT RED UMBRELLA PROJECT

The Red Umbrella Project (RedUP) amplifies the voices of people who have done transactional sex, through media, storytelling, and advocacy programs. We are a small and feisty community-based organization in New York that is peer-led and works to ensure that cisgender and transgender women, cisgender and transgender men, LGBQ people, people who are parents, people of color, people struggling with addictions, people with physical, mental, and emotional disabilities, and people with complex experiences of the sex trade have space to share their experiences with a wide audience, fight discrimination, and use this platform to advocate for change.

Our programs include memoir workshops, improv theater workshops, a monthly storytelling event, a podcast, media and advocacy trainings, and more. We organize campaigns and produce creative projects in collaboration with members of our community in New York.

SUBSCRIBE to PROSE & LORE!

Receive two issues per year of our literary journal in both print and ebook formats, a bookmark, and behind-the-scenes interviews with journal contributors in ebook format.

Subscriptions are $45 a year and are tax deductible.

Learn more about our work and subscribe at redumbrellaproject.org

HUGE THANKS to OUR SUPPORTERS
who help make it possible to publish
PROSE & LORE!

Maria Baldridge
Stacey Harlan
Sheila Moncrief
Olive Seraphim
Marjan Wijers

Want to see your name on this page in future issues? Become a
supporter at sexworkermemoir.org

ALSO PUBLISHED BY
RED UMBRELLA PROJECT

Cooking in Heels: A Memoir Cookbook, by Ceyenne Doroshow with Audacia Ray. Published October 2012.

Prose & Lore, Issue 1, edited by Melissa Petro. Published December 2012.

www.ingramcontent.com/pod-product-compliance
Lightning Source LLC
Chambersburg PA
CBHW072016040426
42447CB00009B/1646